WHITE KNIGHT, RED HEAT
The Many Lives of Benjamin Thompson, Count Rumford

JOHN GRIBBIN

MARY GRIBBIN

 Prometheus Books

Essex, Connecticut

Prometheus Books

An imprint of Globe Pequot, the trade division of The Rowman & Littlefield Publishing Group, Inc.
4501 Forbes Blvd., Ste. 200
Lanham, MD 20706
www.rowman.com

Distributed by NATIONAL BOOK NETWORK

British Library Cataloguing in Publication Information Available

Library of Congress Cataloging-in-Publication Data Available
ISBN 9781633888678 (cloth: alk. paper) | ISBN 9781633888685 (electronic)

♾️™ The paper used in this publication meets the minimum requirements of American National Standard for Information Sciences—Permanence of Paper for Printed Library Materials, ANSI/NISO Z39.48-1992

To engage in experiments on heat was always one of my most agreeable employments.

—Count Rumford, *Mémoires sur la Chaleur*, 1804

I cannot be idle, nor can I amuse myself with moderation. The ardour of my mind is so ungovernable that every object that interests me engages my whole attention, and is pursuid with a degree of indefatigable zeal which approaches to madness.

—Letter to Marc Pictet, 1800

It is certain, that there is nothing more dangerous, in philosophical investigations, than to take any thing for granted, however unquestionable it may appear, till it has been proved by direct and decisive experiment.

—Rumford, *Essay upon the Propagation of Heat in Fluids*, 1797

Thomas Jefferson, Benjamin Franklin, and Count Rumford are the greatest minds that America has produced.

—Franklin D. Roosevelt

CONTENTS

CONTENTS

ACKNOWLEDGMENTS

Any life of Benjamin Thompson must draw heavily on the work of Sanborn Brown, who spent a lifetime studying his life and work, as well as editing the *Collected Works* of Count Rumford.[1] Although our approach to the subject is rather different from his, and (we hope) offers a fresh perspective, we have particularly benefited from being able to "borrow" from him quotations from documents in the United States to which we have not had access. We have also benefited from financial support from the Alfred C. Munger Foundation, and from facilities provided by the University of Sussex, for both of which we are grateful. The Royal Institution, the Royal Society, the British Library, and the Public Record Office provided invaluable access to archive material.

PROLOGUE

Shedding Light on Heat

There is nothing more dangerous in philosophical investigations than to take anything for granted, however unquestionable it may appear, till it has been proved by direct and decisive experiment.
—RUMFORD, "ESSAY UPON THE PROPAGATION OF HEAT"

IN 1797 GRAF VON RUMFORD WAS A SENIOR MEMBER OF THE BAVARIAN aristocracy and adviser to the elector (a kind of prince) who ruled Bavaria from Munich. One of von Rumford's many roles at the height of the turmoil in Europe following the French Revolution was the key post of Inspector General of Artillery for the Bavarian army. In this capacity, he was in charge of the manufacture of cannon at the Munich arsenal, and as he put it in the introduction to a paper read to the Royal Society in London on his behalf on January 25, 1798,[1] as a result "it was by accident that I was led to make the experiments of which I am about to give an account," experiments that are now seen as having laid to rest the caloric theory of heat, and laying the groundwork for the modern kinetic theory, which explains heat as a form of motion, caused by atoms and molecules jostling together. This was one of the most important scientific discoveries of the late eighteenth century. Until that time, it had been widely thought that heat was a kind of fluid, caloric, that could be squeezed out of a substance by pressure. But although the place that von Rumford was in, and the work he was doing, at the time was an accident of revolutionary wars, it was no accident that he noticed something interesting about the process of cannon boring and then, instead of dismissing it as a mere curiosity, carried out careful and accurate scientific experiments to determine what was happening.

Von Rumford's work at the arsenal was of great importance. As he wrote in September 1797, "I have been . . . much employed in casting Cannon and preparing them to be able to give our enemies a warm reception should they pay us another visit. . . . The [French] Jacobins are getting, or rather have gotten the upper hand, and with them it would be folly to expect that peace could exist." To that end, he carried out many experiments with gunpowder, as well as supervised the cannon boring. What he saw convinced him that the caloric theory could not be right.

In the Royal Society paper, he wrote:

Being engaged in superintending the boring of cannon in the work-shops of the military arsenal at Munich, I was struck with the very considerable degree of Heat which a brass gun acquires in a short time in being bored, and with the still more intense Heat (much greater than that of boiling water, as I found by experiment) of the metallic chips separated from it by the borer.

It was well known, of course, that heat could be generated by friction. The explanation, according to the caloric idea, was that the pressure of one object against another squeezed caloric out of the material as they rubbed together, like water being squeezed from a wet sponge. But von Rumford saw that when a brass cylinder was being bored out to make a cannon, there was no decrease in the amount of heat being produced by the friction, no matter how long the process went on—the "sponge" never dried out. Unless the supply of caloric was inexhaustible, which seemed ridiculous, there must be some other explanation for the heat produced by friction.

To demonstrate this, von Rumford devised an experiment in which a blunt drill bit was pressed against a piece of scrap brass on the end of the casting of a cannon—a piece usually cut off before the cannon was bored. This formed a short cylinder just under 10 inches long and 7¾ inches in diameter, joined to the main bulk of the gun by a thin neck of metal. He was at pains to point out that after the experiment the scrap could be cut off and the remaining cylinder bored out in the usual way, so none of the valuable cannon were damaged in the process. The blunt "drill" was fixed, while the cylinder was turned in the usual way by the work of a pair of horses plodding round in a circle, with their harness connected to the drill by gears. In his first series of experiments, von Rumford simply measured the temperature of the air and cylinder at the start, and the temperature of the cylinder after thirty minutes, when it had made 960 revolutions. At the start, the temperature was 60 degrees Fahrenheit; at the end, it had risen to 130 degrees. The "very considerable quantity of Heat" that "actually raised the temperature of above 113 lb. of gun-metal at least 70 degrees" would, von Rumford pointed out, "have been capable of melting 6½ lb. of ice, or of causing near 5 lb. of ice-cold water to boil." This calculation may have inspired the most famous of his cannon-boring experiments.

In this variation, the brass cylinder and the drill bit were enclosed in a wooden box that could be filled with water at 60 degrees, and the machinery set in motion. Setting this up was an exacting task, but "the result of this beautiful experiment was very striking, and the pleasure it afforded me amply repaid me for all the trouble I had had in contriving and arranging the complicated machinery used in making it."

After an hour, the temperature of the water had been raised to 107 degrees, after two hours it was 178 degrees, and "at 2 hours 30 minutes it ACTUALLY BOILED!"[2] "It would be difficult," he said, "to describe the surprise and astonishment expressed in the countenances of the bystanders, on seeing so large a quantity of cold water heated, and actually made to boil, without any fire."

To the further astonishment of those bystanders, in this way von Rumford was able to bring the water in the box to a boil, discard the water, refill the box, and bring it to a boil again, over and over with no sign of the supply of heat running out. "Though there was, in fact, nothing that could justly be considered surprising in this event," von Rumford wrote in his Royal Society paper, "yet I acknowledge fairly that it afforded me a degree of childish pleasure, which, were I ambitious of the reputation of a *grave philosopher*, I ought most certainly rather to hide than to discover."

This was just the most spectacular of a series of experiments in which von Rumford carefully measured the rate at which heat was being produced and carefully weighed all of the metal involved before and after the experiments to see if there were any changes that could be attributed to the loss of caloric. There were not. And yet the amount of heat being produced continually was, he calculated, "*greater* than that produced equably in the combustion of *nine wax candles*, each of ¾ of an inch in diameter, all burning together, or at the same time, with clear bright flames." But he realized that this use of horsepower was not an efficient way to boil water:

> *No circumstances can be imagined in which this method of procuring Heat would not be disadvantageous; for more Heat might be obtained by using the fodder necessary for the support of a horse as fuel.*

With this remark, von Rumford came tantalizingly close to discovering the law of conservation of energy, and with hindsight it also contains the germ of the fundamental principle of thermodynamics, that no process of energy conversion is 100 percent efficient (part of the second law of thermodynamics), so in this case, using hay for food to power the muscles of a horse to generate heat by boring out a brass cylinder is less effective than burning the hay to heat something directly.[3]

All of this reinforced von Rumford's belief that heat is a form of motion. In his own words:

> *It appears to me to be extremely difficult, if not quite impossible, to form any distinct idea of anything capable of being excited and communicated in the manner the Heat was excited and communicated in these experiments, except it be MOTION.*

Although von Rumford confessed that "I am very far from pretending to know how, or by what means or mechanical contrivance, that particular kind of motion in bodies which has been supposed to constitute Heat is excited, continued, and propagated," this is still an impressive conclusion to have reached in 1797. The idea that heat is a form of motion went back at least to the time of Francis Bacon (1561–1626), and the English polymath Robert Hooke (1635–1703) said clearly that it was "nothing else but a brisk and vehement agitation of the parts of a body." But the important feature of von Rumford's work was that rather than arguing the case for the idea, he had proved that the rival caloric idea was wrong. Eliminate the impossible, and whatever was left had to be the truth. As he later wrote,[4] "It has always been impossible for me to explain the results of such experiments except by taking refuge in the very old doctrine which rests on the supposition that heat is nothing but a vibratory motion taking place among the particles of the body." Much later (in 1871), John Tyndall provided the last word on these experiments, commenting that in this memoir Rumford "annihilates the material theory of heat. Nothing more powerful on the subject has since been written."[5]

But who was this Bavarian aristocrat, and why was he getting his hands dirty, as it were, by dabbling in scientific experiments? The truth is that he had not been born into the aristocracy, or even in Bavaria. He had started life as plain Ben Thompson, the son of a farmer in one of the English colonies in North America. The road that took him to Munich was long and adventurous, and 1797 was far from being the end of that road, or the end of his adventures. To follow the story, we must begin, as is traditional, at the beginning.

INTRODUCTION

Tinker, Tailor, Soldier, Spy

BENJAMIN THOMPSON'S LIFE CAN BE NEATLY SUMMED UP IN THE TITLE of John le Carré's novel. But how did a boy who started life as plain Ben Thompson, a farmer's son in Massachusetts in 1753, go on to become a Fellow of the Royal Society, a colonel in the British army (following a spell of spying on their behalf), be knighted by the British, made Minister of War in Bavaria and a count (Graf von Rumford, to be precise) by the Holy Roman Empire, found the Royal Institution in London and "discover" Humphry Davy, then become a leading member of the Institut National de France (while Britain and France were at war!), and end his life in Paris in 1814? Along the way he had literally been a tinker, a tailor, a soldier, and a spy—and much more besides, including a scientist. He was a pioneer in developing the modern understanding of heat, invented a better chimney (still in widespread use) for open fires, and found time to invent the coffee percolator and the enclosed oven. None of this stopped him from having a string of lovers sufficient to form the basis of an entire biography,[1] one of whom, the widow of the great (but guillotined) chemist Pierre-Simon Laplace, became his second wife.

As this brief summary suggests, Thompson/Rumford lived in interesting times that led to his adventurous and varied career. These events included the American War of Independence, the French Revolution, and various wars on the European continent. Several times he escaped disaster by the skin of his teeth, always landing on his feet, with his upward mobility matched by increasing wealth that enabled him, as well as provided comfortably for his own family, to bequeath funds for a professorship at Harvard still active today. Late in life he wrote, "My greatest delight arises from the silent contemplation of having succeeded in schemes and labors for the benefit of mankind."[2] A far cry from life as an eighteenth-century colonial farm boy. Yet that is where our story starts—down on the farm.

PART I
FROM COLONIAL BOY TO BRITISH SPY

CHAPTER I

Colonial Boy

BENJAMIN THOMPSON WAS BORN IN WOBURN, MASSACHUSETTS, A farming community with a population of about 1,500 people, on March 26, 1753. He was descended on the side of his father (another Benjamin Thompson) from James Thompson, a settler who had arrived in New England ten years after the *Mayflower*, in 1630. His father ran the family farm, and his mother, Ruth, was the daughter of an army officer. Young Ben was destined to follow in the footsteps of his grandfather and father and become a farmer, until his father died in November 1754 at the age of twenty-six, when the baby was just twenty months old. Benjamin's grandfather, Ebenezer, outlived his son by a few months, handing the running of the farm over to his younger son, Hiram, and in 1756 young Benjamin's mother remarried (apparently happily), becoming Mrs. Josiah Pierce, and started another family.

But Benjamin was well provided for. He had been left fifty acres of land by his grandfather, who also made it a condition of Hiram taking over the farm that he should pay his nephew 16 shillings a year until he was fourteen, as well as provide for Benjamin's widowed mother until she remarried. Thompson's own accounts of his childhood are colorful and do not always match the facts—as we shall see, he liked embellishing his own biography. In one account, reported by George Ellis, he says, "I was obliged to form the habit of thinking and acting for myself and of depending on my own for a livelihood."[1] This is true up to a point, but he was certainly not left destitute and was given every opportunity, given his family's circumstances, to better himself. He received a good basic

3

education (better than any of the four children of his mother's second marriage) at local schools in Woburn, Byfield, and Medford, where his alertness, aptitude for mathematics, and love of building "mechanical contrivances" were noted.

It may seem surprising that he attended so many "schools," but in towns like Woburn at that time education was a rather haphazard business. The law required that all children should be taught to read and write, and that if the community had more than a hundred families they had to provide a grammar school as well. There were two snags. The farmers didn't set much store by book learning, and the town was too poor to pay a full-time teacher—most trade between the citizens took the form of barter. A schoolmaster was hired only when funds were available, paying lip service to the law, and the "school" was frequently moved to different parts of town to benefit different groups of children. Which is why young Thompson moved from school to school, where his enthusiasm and aptitude contrasted sharply with the reluctant (some sources say "surly") way he carried out his duties back on the farm.

Thompson left school at the age of thirteen, in 1766, but (again, unlike his half-siblings) was given a further opportunity for education and improvement. This came in the form of an apprenticeship, which placed obligations on the master as well as the apprentice. While the apprentice learned his trade, he became in effect part of the master's family and received the same outside opportunities as the children of his host. In Salem, there were plenty of outside opportunities. Although it was just fifteen miles from Woburn, Salem was a bustling port with a cosmopolitan community where the wealthy copied the style and manners of England. The farmers of Woburn had no time for such airs, nor any money to indulge them even if they wished. The people of Salem were by colonial standards well educated, and took an interest in the world outside their own community—most particularly, they were politically aware.

The man Thompson was apprenticed to was a Salem merchant called John Appleton, a graduate of Harvard College who imported goods from England and sold them from his store in the family house. Appleton's ancestors had arrived in America from Suffolk, in England, in 1635, and the family had been pillars of the community ever since. The Appleton family attended the church of the Reverend Thomas Barnard, who had a son roughly the same age as Thompson. The boys became friendly, and through these contacts Barnard, whom Thompson later described as a "very respectable minister," took Thompson under his wing, teaching him algebra, geometry, astronomy, and higher mathematics. He also became, in the words of Ellis, who saw examples of his work, "an able and accurate draughtsman, and an accomplished designer." But this happy relationship did not last, partly because of the changing political situation and partly because of Thompson's own impetuosity.

The political background stemmed from the wars between Britain and France that had essentially ended French control of parts of North America. Fighting between the two colonial powers began on American soil in 1754, and battles took place at various times all the way from Virginia in the south (where a young George Washington was involved on the British side) to Newfoundland in the north. The French colonists were heavily outnumbered by the British and received considerable support from Native American tribes, then referred to as "Indians"; this led to the conflict being given the name by the British of the French and Indian War, even though some tribes supported the British. The war fed in to the much larger European conflict known as the Seven Years' War (1756–1763) and was formally ended by the Treaty of Paris in February 1763, although most of the fighting in America was over in 1760. The treaty reflected the fact that France and her allies lost the war. Britain gained Canada, extensive French territory east of the Mississippi, and (from Spain) Florida. But this came at a cost. The British national debt had nearly doubled as a result of the expenditure on the wars, and the government sought new sources of income in an attempt to balance the books. Not surprisingly, it was felt that the American colonists who had benefited from British efforts to protect them should pay their bit. But the way the government in London set about raising taxes from North America was heavy handed and led to more trouble, at a time when, with the threat from France removed, the need for British protection was less clear to the colonists.

The colonists had, of course, been involved in the fighting, as well as the regular British army. Many of the adult men from Woburn served in the military, but Thompson was not quite seven at the time of the Treaty of Paris so the war largely passed him by. The aftermath of the war, though, directly affected him.

In March 1765 the British Parliament passed a law known as the Stamp Act, which would come into force the following November. This essentially required anything printed, such as contracts or legal documents, newspapers, other publications, and even playing cards, to carry a stamp purchased from the British authorities. Worse, the tax had to be paid with British currency, not the paper used among the colonists, although it was stipulated that the funds would also be spent in the colonies, for example, on the upkeep of the army. It was the first direct tax imposed on the American colonies and provoked the famous response "no taxation without representation" because the colonists did not elect members of Parliament to Westminster. The protesters did not stop with words. When news of the tax reached America, it triggered violent demonstrations in the colonies and a deputation to London, led by Benjamin Franklin, to make their case. Franklin told the House of Commons that if the act were not repealed there would be "a total loss of the respect and affection the people of America bear to this country, and of all the commerce that depends on that respect and affection."

After these strong protests the act was repealed, with effect from May 1766, although this was coupled with a declaration from the British Parliament asserting its supremacy over the colonies "in all cases whatsoever." This was followed up with plans for new taxes and laws controlling the American colonies.

This was the first step toward what became either the American Revolution or the War of Independence, depending on which side you were on, and the situation that existed when Benjamin Thompson, aged thirteen, began his new life in Salem. There was a groundswell of anti-government feeling (not necessarily anti-British) and a desire to make London listen to the wishes of the colonies. One way to make London sit up and take notice would be to stop importing British goods, which would hit the British economy. Unfortunately, though, a ban on British goods would also affect the colonial economy. Either out of patriotism or under pressure from activists who had less to lose personally, John Appleton gave a solemn undertaking not to import any more goods from Great Britain, and his business went into decline just as he was taking on a new apprentice. This would probably have led to Appleton being forced to give up the arrangement, but before that could happen Thompson unintentionally brought things to a head in the summer of 1769 by blowing himself up and damaging part of the store while making fireworks (possibly intended to be used as part of a celebration of the anniversary of the repeal of the Stamp Act). He was badly burned and sent home to Woburn to recuperate. Thompson spun out the "recuperation" as long as possible, continuing his program of self-improvement, in collaboration with a similarly inclined older friend, a near neighbor in Woburn called Loammi Baldwin. Baldwin kept many letters and documents concerning his relationship with Thompson; these were a key source for the biography by Ellis.

The two must have become friends well before Thompson went to Salem, but the first record we have of their interaction comes from a letter Thompson wrote to Baldwin from Salem in 1768. Baldwin was nine years older than Thompson but seems to have been at about the same level of education. He worked with his father, a carpenter, and had only attended local schools to learn the basics of reading, writing, and arithmetic, but, like Thompson, he was eager to better himself, and he would go on to become one of the leading engineers in the state of Massachusetts. At this time, they provided ideal foils for one another, bouncing questions to and fro and competing to find the answers. Jumping ahead of our narrative a little, we can get a glimpse of this collaboration from letters Thompson wrote to Baldwin in 1769. He posed questions about the way light is reflected; the change in color of clay when heated; how fire "operates upon Silver, to change it to Blue"; and the "Rise of the Wind." Long after, when Thompson became famous as Count Rumford, Baldwin recalled that one night the younger man had walked the fifteen miles each way from Salem to Woburn to show him a "perpetual motion machine" that he had designed.

After putting up with Benjamin's recuperation for what seems a generous amount of time, Thompson's stepfather's patience ran out, and he "suggested" that it was time for the young man to get a proper job. This involved a move to Boston. In October 1769 Hopestill Capen, the owner of a store in that town, wrote to John Appleton requesting a reference for Thompson. We do not have a copy of Appleton's reply, but it must have been favorable because a few days later Thompson wrote to Appleton to thank him for providing a recommendation, and he soon started work in the building that was then called "The Sign of the Cornfields."[2] His motivation, it is clear, was much more the opportunity to move to Boston than a wish to become a clerk in a dry-goods store, living in an attic above the shop. In correspondence with Benjamin's mother Capen sorrowfully recounts how her son was more likely to be found underneath the counter reading a science book or making some little machine than standing behind it serving the customers. He was also fond of playing the violin. Thompson's real interests lay outside the store, where there were many private "schools" (often actually individual tutors) offering evening classes for self-improvers like Thompson. He definitely signed up for lessons in French and in fencing, and possibly for other classes.

Capen was loyal to the British crown, and with a strong British presence in Boston he had no trouble getting a market for his goods, and no compunction about buying them from Great Britain. But the winds of change were not blowing in his favor. Opponents of the British army's presence frequently harassed the soldiers with jeering and name calling, and on the night of March 5, 1770, one of these minor incidents blew up into something worse. A mob surrounded a British sentry and started catcalling. When eight other soldiers came to his aid they were struck with clubs, stones, and snowballs. Overreacting to the situation, they fired into the crowd, killing three people and wounding others; two of the victims later died of their wounds. This became known to Americans as the Boston Massacre, and to the British as the Incident on King Street. Although two of the soldiers were found guilty of manslaughter, and there was clearly provocation, the "incident" provided ideal propaganda material for the antiroyalists; John Adams[3] later wrote that the "foundation of American independence was laid" on that day. But while

Boston was in turmoil, Thompson was soon back on the farm. Apparently having been sacked by Capen, he returned to Woburn in the spring of 1770 and earned a little money in the months that followed by cutting firewood on the land he had inherited and selling it around the community. This left plenty of time for philosophizing with Loammi Baldwin and self-education.

Part of this process, we learn from Thompson's later writings, involved reading, "in my seventeenth year," the comprehensive treatise on chemistry written by Herman Boerhaave (1668–1738),[4] which included a lengthy chapter on heat. "To engage in experiments on heat was always one of my most agreeable employments," he wrote in 1804;[5] this was, indeed, the field in which he made his greatest contribution to science, so this early interest is a significant pointer to the future. But Thompson's next attempt at self-advancement took a rather different turn, which seemed at first sight well suited to his talents. He became apprenticed to the local physician in Woburn, Dr. John Hay. But he never seriously devoted himself to medicine, and the apprenticeship did not last long; he was the kind of person who worked far harder at things he was interested in, for no financial reward, than he ever did as a paid employee.

Thompson continued to investigate science with Loammi Baldwin, accompanying him in June 1771 on the eight-mile walk to Harvard College in Cambridge, where for a few days they sat in, unofficially, on lectures by Professor John Winthrop about what was then still called "experimental philosophy"—in other words, physics. Probably inspired by Winthrop's lecture on electricity, there was an attempt to construct (among other things) an electrical apparatus similar to a Van de Graaff generator, and more alarmingly an attempt to replicate Benjamin Franklin's famous kite-flying experiment, in July 1771. According to Baldwin's account, this resulted in him being engulfed in "the midst of a large bright flame of fire" while feeling "a general weakness of my joints and limbs and a kind of listless feeling." This "was sufficient to discourage me from any further attempts."

Thompson's diary records the schedule he set for himself at this time:

Munday—Anatomy

Tewsday—Anatomy

Wednesday—Institutes of Physic

Thurdsday—Surgery

Fryday—Chimistry with the Materia Medica

Saturday—Physick 1/2 and Surgery 1/2

He also wrote out a rigid timetable of daily activities, beginning with exercise and study from 6 a.m. until 8 a.m., followed by breakfast and prayers, more study from 10 until noon, lunch, "constant" study from 1 to 4, an hour for relaxation, and an evening spent doing "what my inclination Leads me to." Even more enlighteningly, Thompson's notebooks contain the exhortation "never allow an opportunity of advancement to escape me." This is an early example of Thompson's obsession with lists and order, a characteristic that he shared with some other great scientists, and has led to speculation that a tendency toward mild autism might be an asset in probing the mysteries of the universe.

Thompson certainly lived his life by the creed "never allow an opportunity of advancement to escape me," but whether he stuck to this ambitious program of self-improvement as an apprentice doctor we will never know. His attitude to medicine is perhaps summed up by an anecdote in the records of the New Hampshire Historical Society:[6]

> *Returning home one day [Dr Hay] was much surprised at hearing a hog squealing up chamber, ran up, in great haste. Behold, Thompson had got the bronchia of a hog, blowing into them.*

We don't know if such high jinks were typical. What we do know is that Thompson struggled financially at this time and had difficulty finding the 40 shillings a week to pay Dr. Hay for his lodgings and tuition in medicine. This led to his next change of career path. He interrupted his medical apprenticeship twice, in the winter of 1771 and the spring of 1772, to take temporary employment as a schoolteacher, teaching the basics of reading, writing, and arithmetic. The second of these jobs was in Bradford, Massachusetts, in March and April 1772, where he made the acquaintance of the minister Reverend Samuel Williams, who was a serious scholar with a special interest in history as well as being a churchman. He was impressed by the young man, and seems to have been instrumental in convincing him that his vocation lay in teaching, not in medicine. The apprenticeship was terminated by mutual consent (and probably to Dr. Hay's relief) in June 1772, and the nineteen-year-old Ben Thompson moved to Bradford to study with Williams and learn some schoolteaching from the regular schoolmaster there, Timothy Walker, while trying to find a suitable post.[7]

Just about the only requirements for a schoolteacher in the colonies in those days was that he could actually read, write, and reckon himself. Communities in need of a teacher would put the word out, and a committee of leading citizens would select who they considered to be the best man for the job. In 1772, the village—it was scarcely a town—of Concord, New Hampshire, was looking for a schoolteacher, and the most important man in town was the Reverend Timothy Walker, a cousin of the schoolmaster in Bradford, whose family came from Woburn and knew Thompson. Through this connection, and the good offices of Williams and the Reverend Timothy Walker, Thompson was offered the job.

The community now known as Concord, New Hampshire, had been an early settlement, and was incorporated as Rumford in 1733 by Massachusetts. The original name is thought to have reflected the fact that early settlers came from Romford, in Essex. But in 1741, after a dispute about the border line, it was decided that the town was within the Province of New Hampshire, not Massachusetts. This triggered a bitter legal fight that went all the way to the Privy Council in England, and the dispute was not settled until 1762. In 1765 the town formally became part of New Hampshire and was renamed Concord as a gesture of reconciliation to the parties involved in the dispute. So Concord had born its name for less than ten years in August 1772 when a tall, handsome young man of nineteen rode into town to take up lodgings in the household of the Reverend Timothy Walker and take up his duties as schoolmaster.[8]

Reverend Walker, a widower, was an important man in Concord, wealthy enough in his own right to own three slaves, in spite of his position as a churchman. He had been born in 1705, graduated from Harvard College in 1725, and settled in the community (then known as the plantation of Penacook) in 1730, as their first minister. In the years that followed, the people in the plantation had to contend with hostile natives, wolves, and a plague of rattlesnakes, as well as the arguments about boundaries and who was entitled to collect local taxation from the plantation. Even by 1772, it was a small village, less than half the size of Woburn, not much more than a backwoods settlement.

Alongside Reverend Walker, the other leading citizen of Concord had until recently been Benjamin Rolfe, a wealthy landowner and a full colonel in the New Hampshire militia. He had been born in 1710, graduated from Harvard in 1727, and inherited large amounts of land, which he added to over the years. He was active in the militia and over the years held every important administrative post in the community. When his health started to fail in 1769, he made careful plans for the future. He resigned his post as town clerk in favor of Walker's son, Timothy Walker Junior, and in an arrangement to ensure that his wealth passed into Walker's family he married the daughter of Reverend Walker, Sarah, who was some thirty years his junior—born on October 6, 1739, she was almost exactly half his age. They had a son, Paul, born on August 4, 1770, but in December 1771 Colonel Rolfe died, leaving Sarah as the richest widow in New Hampshire. Eight months later, Thompson arrived in the household.

The school he took charge of was surprisingly large. In a letter to his mother, he reported that there were officially 106 "Scholars," but that, for the reasons we outlined earlier, there were generally only about seventy in attendance at any one time. Nevertheless, Concord was even more of a backwater than Woburn, and Thompson had been trying to get away to the brighter lights of somewhere like Salem or Boston for years. It is unlikely that he would have stayed long, but an even better opportunity than schoolmastering fell into his lap. Seemingly following his dictum "never allow an opportunity of advancement to escape me," in November 1772, less than four months after arriving in Concord, Benjamin

Thompson married the widow of Colonel Rolfe—although in later life he always said that "she married me, not I her," suggesting that she felt he was a better bet than being the widowed single mother of a baby boy living with her elderly father. The fact that she had been unmarried at thirty (an old maid by the standards of the day), then settled for an arranged marriage with her father's best friend when he was on his last legs suggests that she must have been no beauty, and if not desperate then certainly concerned about her future. Thompson's appearance at this time has been described by Baldwin:[9]

> *Of fine, manly make and figure, nearly six feet high, with handsome features, bright blue eyes and dark auburn hair. His manners were polished and his ways fascinating, and he could well make himself agreeable. He had well used his opportunities of culture, so that his knowledge was beyond that of most of those around him.*

Whatever the truth about who pursued whom, it is clear that Thompson must have been a charming, articulate, and self-confident young man with polished manners, and the Reverend Walker gave the union his blessing. All thoughts of schoolteaching were forgotten, and Thompson became a member of the landed gentry.

As such, the most obvious thing he lacked to suit his new position was fine clothing. So a few weeks before the wedding, in the autumn of 1772, nineteen-year-old Benjamin and thirty-three-year-old Sarah went on a trip with two objectives—to Boston to fit him out with appropriate finery, and to Woburn to break the news of his engagement to Thompson's mother. The first part of the trip went well. They traveled in a two-horse curricle, the equivalent of a modern drop head sports car,[10] and one of only two in the entire Province of New Hampshire—the other was owned by the governor. If this isn't enough to give you an idea of Thompson's tastes, the clothing should. The purchases featured a cloak faced in scarlet, to supplement the marginally more modest blue "Hussar" cloak that he had bought just a year earlier with money earned from selling wood. The second part of the trip started off badly. When Thompson rolled up in Woburn dressed in scarlet, riding in a fancy carriage and with an older woman at his side, his mother took some persuading that the woman and the relationship were respectable. They obtained her blessing only after she had slept on the news and taken in the fact that her son was about to marry the richest woman in New Hampshire.

The wedding took place on November 14, 1772, less than eleven months after the death of Sarah's first husband; whether by accident or design the timing provided Thompson with another opportunity of advancement. There was a grand military review of the 2nd Provincial Regiment of New Hampshire—the militia—at Dover, near Portsmouth (then the capital of New Hampshire) on November 13, 1772. The governor, John Wentworth, one of Sarah's relatives, invited the couple to attend. Thompson didn't just attend; he took the opportunity to ride past the regiment and the other observers, resplendent in his scarlet cloak, on a fine white horse. The festivities moved on to Portsmouth, where the wedding took place, and the happy couple were invited to dinner that evening at the governor's house. Thompson was sounded out about his political leanings, and within a few months, after proving useful to the governor, he was offered the rank of major in the militia; the commission was dated January 20, 1774. It was the next step in his upwardly mobile progress. As Thompson said much later to his friend Marc Auguste Pictet, a source[11] of many anecdotes (not always reliable) about his early years,

> *I was launched at the right time upon a world which was strange to me, and I was obliged to form the habit of thinking and acting for myself . . . perhaps I should have acquired a habit of indecision and inconstancy, perhaps I should have been poor and unhappy all my life, if a woman had not loved me—if she had not given me a subsistence, a home, an independent fortune.*

His appointment in the militia wasn't quite the blatant act of nepotism it may seem, and Wentworth had good reasons to make Thompson his protégé. Wentworth was nobody's fool. He was part of the colonial establishment, a member of the group of families who had made fortunes in America in the seventeenth and eighteenth centuries, and who were the accepted rulers of provinces. Born in Portsmouth, New Hampshire, he had graduated from Harvard College and spent three years in England being groomed for greatness by the Marquis of Rockingham, where he took part in the successful campain to repeal the Stamp Act. He also found time to obtain a degree in law from the University of Oxford, and he became governor of New Hampshire in August 1766. Wentworth was intelligent, well read, and well liked, and a very able governor, who opposed the heavy-handed aproach of the government in London and stood up for the rights of the colonists. He took an interest in science, and had his duties permitted he would have liked to explore the White Mountains to the west, the boundary of the region inhabited by Europeans. In January 1773, Thompson proposed his own scientific expedition to the mountains, which involved him in further contact with the governor. From what we know of Thompson, the motivation for the proposal was probably a combination of his genuine interest in the world beyond the boundaries of civilization and a chance to become on even better terms with Wentworth. But the plan eventually came to nothing because of the changing political situation. And it was the changing political situation that made the appointment of Thompson as a major in the militia desirable.

To put this in perspective, we should emphasize that Thompson was a loyal British subject. He later said that "from principle I supported the king because I considered this to be the lawful attitude."[12] All the colonists were British subjects of course, but some were more loyal than others. Thompson's loyalty to the crown may have been partly due to his natural inclination (as his comment indicates, he was a conservative, with a small *c*) and partly due to his new status in society; but it is worth bearing in mind that in the years of turmoil that followed there were several occasions when pure self-interest would have led Thompson down a different path from the one he actually followed.

Thompson's usefulness to Wentworth began when the governor ran into trouble with the Board of Trade in London. The trouble began because Wentworth was too honest. His predecessor as governor of New Hampshire had been his uncle, Benning Wentworth, who had awarded large tracts of land to cronies in an illegal manner. When John

Wentworth declared these titles null and void, his uncle's cronies stirred up trouble in London, claiming that he had dispossessed them, although in fact nobody had ever made any effort to improve the land, which was a condition of such charters. The grandly titled Lords of Trade recommended to the Privy Council that Wentworth should be dismissed, but his appeal against this decision was successful in no small part because he submitted testimonials including an elaborate "Address of the Inhabitents of Concord" that in fine language extolled the virtues of the governor and concluded that were the facts of the dispute

> *Represented in a True point of Light, we are fully satisfied that [the Governor] would receive the Approbation of His Majesty, and the Applause of the People of this Province in general.*

Although it was signed by the town clerk of Concord, the address was written by Thompson. In September 1773, Wentworth was formally exonerated; on January 20, 1774, as we have mentioned, Thompson became a major in the militia.

By then, he was becoming established in his role as a member of the landed gentry. Thompson had thrown himself enthusiastically into the scientific management of his estates and husbandry—as we shall see, he threw himself enthusiastically into everything he attempted. A list of seed goods he ordered from England included best red clover, five kinds of cabbage, four varieties of turnip, and six kinds of peas, as well as many varieties of oats, barley, and wheat. He never got to plant any of these, let alone find out which varieties were best on his land, but it is easy to imagine that if things had worked out differently he might have built on his wife's inheritance, strengthened his political contacts, and in all probability become the next governor of New Hampshire. But by 1774 there was already widespread civil disturbance throughout the colonies, and an increasing need for a well-regulated militia, necessary for the security of the state. Thompson was part of the Fifteenth Regiment of Militia, which included several senior officers with military experience; his role was mainly organizational, involving recruitment for the new regiment. By June 1774 the regiment was complete, with fifteen companies, each

headed by a captain, lieutenant, and ensign; below them came the ser-
geants. In the whole regiment, there were no privates. This, though, was
just the visible aspect of Thompson's work on behalf of the military. It was
his undercover work, detailed in the next chapter, that triggered the next
dramatic change in his life.

In October 1774, Thompson became the father of a daughter, Sally.
This should have set the seal on his succesful transition from colonial boy
to officer and gentleman. But by that time simply being a loyal British
citizen and a friend of the governor was itself enough to rouse suspicion
and hostility in the minds of most of the colonists—and there was plenty
more than that for them to be suspicious about. This was almost the end
of happy days in Concord, and in effect of his marriage.

CHAPTER 2

British Spy

BY DECEMBER 1774, REVOLUTION WAS IN THE AIR. IN 1773, A TAX imposed on tea had led to the famous "Boston Tea Party" of December 16, when a group of colonists dressed up ("disguised" is too strong a word) as Native Americans raided three ships in Boston Harbor and threw their cargoes of tea overboard. This act was symbolically important to both sides, although the situation was more complicated than many popular accounts suggest. When the government in London had removed other taxes, in 1769, they kept the tax on tea as a symbol of their right to impose taxation; but initially the local tax paid by the Americans was just part of a larger pattern of tea taxes. For four years, the tax was paid, if only grudgingly. In 1773, however, the prime minister, Lord North, removed all the other taxes, allowing the British East India Company to sell tea to America "free of all English customs and excise duties" but still subject to an import duty in America. This was actually intended by Lord North not only as a favor to the East India Company but, by reducing the cost of tea, as a concession to the colonists. They saw it differently. Now they were the only people paying a tax on the imported tea, singled out, as they saw it, for victimization by the British. The "tea party" was a symbolic rejection of the principle that the British had a right to impose taxes in this way. The British response was to close the port of Boston and make Salem the capital of Massachusetts, while passing a series of acts that imposed a semimilitary rule and required citizens of Boston to house British soldiers in their homes. The colonists' response was the First Continental Congress, in September 1774, attended by representatives of all thirteen colonies except Georgia. This called for civil disobedience and the repeal of the new acts and led to the setting up of a volunteer militia force, ostensibly to be available at a minute's notice and therefore called the Minutemen.

The British response to the unrest had included sacking the American-born governor of Massachusetts, Thomas Hutchinson, and replacing him with a hard man from England, General Thomas Gage, who took over in Boston in May 1774. Gage was a military man sent to use force if necessary to crush a rebellion, in marked contrast to both his predecessor and Wentworth, who had tried conciliation and listening to the will of the people—people who were their neighbors and whom they had known all their lives. But the confusion of the times is highlighted by the fact that Gage was married to a colonial and owned land in America. He regarded his role as essentially a police action, expecting things to return to normal once the troublesome element had been dealt with. Thompson clearly thought much the same way. With limited resources at his disposal, Gage had to call on reinforcements from neighboring provinces, which up to that point had been quieter than Massachusetts. This involved close contact with Wentworth, and through him Thompson was drawn in to Gage's network of contacts and spies.

In readiness for the anticipated clash with British forces, the colonists were building up their own forces of trained men, ready to fight. But to do this they needed instructors with military experience, and they got them by inducing soldiers to desert from the British army. Citizens of provinces such as New Hampshire promised deserters their own farmland, as well as generous pay while they were acting as instructors. Many found the attraction irresistible. To counter this loss of men, Wentworth and Thompson, with Gage's collaboration, devised a cunning scheme. Thompson now owned large amounts of land, and he genuinely needed a large force of men to work the land. He hired anyone who came looking for work, but if he found out they were deserters he made their working conditions so miserable that many decided they had been better off in the army. One of Thompson's field hands was actually a British regular, William Bowdidge, working for Gage. He would tell these discontents that he could fix a free pardon, and also square things with Thompson, if they went back to Boston. The scheme worked beautifully in the summer of 1774, to such an extent that Wentworth told Rockingham that many men had rejoined their regiments "with such ideas of the Country as will effectually deter others or themselves from repeating the experiment."[1] As a result of this success, Thompson became known to Gage, whom he met early in November that year. And his own name began to appear in official dispatches. Wentworth reported to London that

> *I have been successful in prevailing on soldiers deserted from the King's troops at Boston, to return to their duty, thro' the spirited and prudent activity of Major Thompson, a Militia officer of New Hampshire: whose management, the General writes me, promises further success.*[2]

But the bubble was about to burst. In the autumn of 1774 two deserters were found hiding out in the town of Boscawen, not far from Concord. They were offered a free pardon, by Thompson himself, and promised to return to Boston. Then they changed their minds. Thompson sent Bowdidge to browbeat them into submission, but an angry mob surrounded Bowdidge and sent him packing. To get him out of harm's way, Thompson sent Bowdidge back to Boston. Although the two deserters pointed the finger at Thompson, he denied everything, and they had no witnesses to back up their claim that he had offered them a pardon on behalf of General Gage. But suspicion was growing, and this was the beginning of the end of Thompson's activity in Concord. A few weeks later, a man from Concord happened to run into Bowdidge, dressed in his British army uniform, in Boston. Back home, this discovery led to the convening of a "Committee of Correspondence," a kind of kangaroo court, that summoned Thompson to answer charges of being a "Rebel to the State" and "unfriendly to the cause of Liberty." The meeting took place on December 12, 1774.

The case was dismissed for lack of evidence—"not proven," rather than "not guilty." Dissatisfied, two days later an angry mob descended on Thompson's house. They may have been planning no more than a noisy demonstration, heckling and banging pots and pans, known as a shivaree. Or they may have been intending to tar and feather Thompson and run him out of town. Thompson was taking no chances. He had been warned in advance of the existence of the mob and had already fled, helped by his brother-in-law Timothy Walker, who gave him $20 and a fast horse to speed him on his way. He left Sarah, her father, and the baby to face the music. Thompson went initially to Charlestown near Boston, then on to Boston itself.

From the safety of Charlestown, Thompson wrote a long and revealing letter, now in the archive of the New Hampshire Historical Society, to his father-in-law:

> *Nothing short of the most threat'ning danger could ever have induced me to leave my Friends & Family. . . . I must humbly beg your kind care of my distressed Family. And hope you will take opportunity to alleviate their trouble, by assuring them that I am in a place of safety. . . . [T]his you may rely & depend on, that I never did, nor (let my treatment be what it will) ever will, do any action that may have the most distant tendency to injure the true interest of this my native Country.*

This demonstrates Thompson's skill with words. We know from his later words and actions that he was a loyal British citizen and royalist. He saw the "true interest" of his native country to lie in being loyal to the crown and the government in London. But if his friends and relations in Concord chose to read his words differently, they could see them as a denial of the charges brought against him by the Committee of Correspondence. This dichotomy also highlights a feature of the war that followed that is often overlooked. Both sides in the conflict were British citizens. There were many back in England who, like Rockingham, sympathized with the cause of the colonists, and many in the colonies who, like Thompson, were loyal to the government in London. In party political terms, the loyalists were Tory, and the rebel sympathizers Whig. Depending on your point of view, what is usually known as the American War of Independence could be regarded either as the last English civil war or the first American civil war.[3]

When Thompson arrived in Boston at the end of 1774, Gage was in desperate need of intelligence about the forces being gathered by the colonists. Although as yet there were no open hostilities, the town was just about the only place where British rule prevailed. Gage controlled this military base, but had very little influence over what went on in the country outside. Anyone who was familiar with the area and did not have an easily identified British accent was welcomed into an intelligence-gathering organization being run by Gage's brother-in-law, Colonel Stephen Kemble. Thompson became Kemble's prime asset. He was a local man, had some military experience, and had already proved his loyalty at considerable risk to his own safety. He was the ideal person to act as a courier for Gage's top spy, Benjamin Church.

Church was not a loyalist and was strictly in it for the money. He was actually a leading figure among the Massachusetts Whigs, having graduated from Harvard in 1754 and studied medicine in London before returning with his English wife to practice in Massachusetts. He served on several important Provincial committees, and was highly respected. But he had an extravagant lifestyle that included an expensive mistress, and to help fund this, by 1744 if not earlier he was being given a quarterly retainer by Gage for information supplied. The problem was how to get the information from Church in Watertown to Gage in Boston without drawing attention to the relationship, and this is where Thompson came in. He was able to travel freely, maintaining the appearance of a country gentleman, unjustly accused of being "unfriendly to the cause of Liberty," keeping his head down and waiting for the situation to be resolved.

Thompson's activities on behalf of Colonel Kemble did not stop there, and in what would be a recurring theme throughout his life, in Boston he found a way to mix business with pleasure. All the evidence suggests that his wife Sarah was Thompson's first sexual partner, but she was certainly not the last. For just over three months Thompson lived in Boston not far from the premises of Isaiah Thomas, who was the proprietor and printer of a revolutionary newspaper, *The Massachusetts Spy*. Thomas and his wife Mary lived on the premises, and revolutionary activists often met there to make plans. Mary, who was in the old expression "no better than she should have been," had a colorful past, was neglected by her husband while he plotted revolution, and found the handsome young major living just round the corner irresistible. This is more than mere speculation. In 1777 Thomas divorced his wife, and the records in the Boston Court House contain his testimony that "at divers times in the month of February, Anno Domini 1775, the said Mary hath been surpriz'd in such familiarities with one Major Thompson to give the strongest Reason to suspect that she was guilty of Adultery with the said Thompson." Her husband also reported that Mary told him that she would "roast in Hell rather than give him [Thompson] up." The affair undoubtedly provided Thompson with information about what she had overheard from the plotters, who included Paul Revere. But this flow of intelligence stopped in April 1775, when Thompson was on a visit to his mother in Woburn at the time the shooting war began.

On April 19, 1775, a force of about seven hundred British soldiers was sent to destroy a rebel military supply dump at Concord. The colonists had got wind of the raid and removed the supplies, while a force of about five hundred of their militia met the British at Lexington. It was there that the first shots were fired, but the outnumbered colonists were forced to retreat, and the British reached Concord, where their search for the supplies proved fruitless. Meanwhile the colonial militia had been reinforced and regrouped, and defeated the British at the Battle of North Bridge, immortalized in Ralph Waldo Emerson's "Concord Hymn," which begins:

By the rude bridge that arched the flood,

Their flag to April's breeze unfurled,
Here once the embattled farmers stood,
And fired the shot heard round the world.[4]

The British were forced to retreat to the region of old Boston situated on a peninsula connected to the mainland by a narrow neck of land. This was easy to defend, but also easily blockaded by the rebels, leaving the British in Boston in a full state of siege—and coincidentally leaving Thompson cut off from them in Woburn. But although it was now impossible for Thompson, suspected of British sympathies, to travel in person in and out of Boston, some contact was maintained, and it was possible, though not easy, to get letters carried into the town.

A couple of weeks later, on May 6, 1775, Thompson sent an innocent-looking letter to a contact in Boston. The letter was laid out in widely spaced writing, with large blank spaces between the lines. The blank spaces in the letter contained a message written in invisible ink, which the British, then under the command of Thomas Gage, developed and read; it is still in the British archives, and contains information about the rebel army (the term used by Thompson) being raised in New England and its plans to attack Boston. Had its contents been discovered by the "rebel army," Thompson would certainly have been tried and hanged, which gives the lie to suggestions that Thompson was merely an adventurer acting in his own self-interest. But by the standards of the day, the secret writing (the earliest surviving example of such a letter from the conflict) was highly technologically sophisticated.

Around this time, Thompson complained widely that he was suffering from diarrhea, a common complaint at the time, which the colonists treated with an infusion made from nut galls, lumps produced on oak twigs where insects have laid their eggs. So it was natural that Thompson should have this infusion in his rooms. But the liquid also has another property. It is a very pale yellow color, and if used to write on the slightly yellowish paper of the day leaves no mark visible to the eye. But if the paper is soaked in a solution of iron sulfate a reaction occurs that makes the writing visible. In this way, Thompson passed his news to General Gage, through an intermediary, without the rebels being aware.

The message he conveyed, some seven hundred words long, was crucially important. It not only gave Gage an indication of the size of the forces being raised against him, but informed him that the rebels planned a diversionary attack on Boston to cover a main assault on a fort on Castle Island, the main base from which the British sent out troops on raids like the fruitless attempt to capture military equipment at Concord. He ends by saying:

As to my own situation, it has been very disagreeable since I left Boston, as upon my refusing to bear Arms against the King I was more than ever suspected by the People in this part of the Country. And it has been with difficulty that the few friends that I have here more than once prevented my bein Assasinated.

Where did Thompson's information come from? In large measure, from conversations with one of those "few friends"—Loammi Baldwin, who was now a major in George Washington's growing army,[5] but remained on good terms with Thompson, who held the same rank in the militia. Their relationship developed over the next few weeks in a way that looks bizarre to modern eyes but highlights the confusion and conflicts of interest associated with the American War of Independence.

In the second week of May, Thompson was again accused of being "enemical to the Liberties of this Country" and held awaiting a formal hearing. Clearly reasoning that attack was the best form of defense, Thompson campaigned vigorously for a public hearing, writing to the commander in chief of the local militias, General Artemas Ward, and soliciting testimonials from friends and officers of his own Fifteenth Regiment. A hearing was held on May 18, where nothing was proved against Thompson, but rather than actually acquitting him the meeting was adjourned, leaving him in limbo. After more campaigning, the committee met again on May 29 and decided that they felt "bound to dismiss [the charges] and recommend the said Thompson unless something more appears against him than what they have heard." It was hardly a ringing endorsement, but Thompson was again free to move around Woburn and the surrounding region. He was also free from another commitment, although this did not immediately become clear.

We don't know when they arrived in Woburn, but while all this was going on Thompson's wife and daughter were staying with him. They left for Concord at the end of May or early in June, after he had received the grudging endorsement of the local Committee of Correspondence. He would never see his wife again and he would not see his daughter Sally until decades had passed and he was living in what amounted to another world.

There is a curious postscript to the story. In Baldwin's papers there was a document dated May 29 purporting to come from the Woburn Committee of Correspondence, issuing a warmer endorsement, concluding that they "do not find that said Thompson in any one instance has shown a Disposition unfriendly to American Liberty," and "we recommend him to the Friendship, Confidence, and Protection of all good People in this and the neighbouring Provinces—Colonies." No such document was made public at the time, and the surmise is that it was a draft prepared by Baldwin in the hope of obtaining the approval of the committee for its publication.

Even without this, Thompson was now free and well placed to continue spying on behalf of the British. His formal status as an officer in the militia was the same as that of the officers in what might by now be regarded as Washington's regular army, but he had no army duties. His cover was that he was eager to become one of those regular officers, but that the unjustified suspicions of the New Hampshire people and the less than ringing endorsement of the Committee of Correspondence made this impossible at the time. He also ostentatiously made himself useful—or gave the appearance of trying to make himself useful—by designing and offering to have manufactured epaulets for the noncommissioned officers of the embryonic army, to distinguish them from the common soldiers. This fitted a genuine need because the army lacked uniforms. Thompson persuaded Baldwin to show the prototypes to Washington. This may have been simply an attempt to profit from the situation, or a ploy to demonstrate his loyalty to the rebel cause, or (most likely judging from his later career) a bit of both.

Baldwin, as this implies, was himself now well placed in Washington's army. He was promoted to colonel, and was acting as an intelligence agent, gathering information about the situation in Boston from contacts there who were able to send letters out by boat. At the same time, in the summer of 1775, his close friend Thompson was doing the same thing in reverse, gathering information about the rebel army for the British, and smuggling it in the opposite direction. As Ellis, who never suspected Thompson of being a British spy, innocently comments, "He strolled between Woburn, Medford, Cambridge and Charlestown, learning whatever his inquisitive and inquiring mind could appropriate." Bizarrely, the two friends often went about this work together, strolling around to look at military encampments, fortifications, and shipbuilding activity. For example, on June 4 Baldwin wrote in his diary:[6]

> *At noon went down to see the [British] Men-of-War fire, &c. to Lechmere point, and viewed Boston &c. Major Thompson and Lieut. Reed was my company.*

It is inconceivable that Baldwin, who had known Thompson since childhood, did not know what his friend was up to, and because Baldwin had no reason to hide his role as a loyal officer in Washington's army, it is inconceivable that Thompson did not know what Baldwin was up to. Brown suggests that they were each hoping to glean information from the other, what he describes as "a dangerous but not uncommon game among espionage and counterespionage agents"; if so, Thompson must have benefited much more from the tacit understanding than Baldwin did. When he returned to Boston in November, as we describe shortly, he produced an exhaustive report for the British that still survives in the archives. This doesn't just cover the obvious things like the state of fortifications, location of powder magazines, and number of cannon available to the rebels but goes into details about morale, the health of Washington's soldiers, politics, discipline, and morale. He correctly describes the soldiers as "wretchedly" clothed and dirty, and so committed to the principle of equality (referred to by him as "levellism") that soldiers were reluctant to take orders. But he seems to have missed recognizing that in spite of all this there was a fierce enthusiasm for fighting the British. He also advised on strategy and tactics. Boats that were being gathered in sight of the Boston shore were, he said, only a diversion, put there to ensure that the garrison in Boston stayed on the alert for an attack instead of "going to distant parts of the Country to Ravage." And he reported on the spread of a typhoid epidemic through New England. When the disease struck among the soldiers, victims were sent home (basically, to die), which had the effect of spreading the disease across the country. Thompson was one of the victims, succumbing in August, but recovering by the autumn.

By then, his plans to leave Woburn were well advanced. While he was recovering from typhoid, in late August, Thompson became concerned about incriminating papers that he had left in Boston and that were increasingly at risk of being discovered by rebel sympathizers. The papers were in a trunk that he had left behind in his lodgings in April, expecting to be able to return shortly. When his landlady also left Boston, the trunk was given to a Mrs. Cromartie to look after, but Thompson did not trust her, and wrote to the Reverend Samuel Parker, one of Boston's leading Tories, asking his urgent help in securing the trunk. The letter, presumably smuggled in by boat, says that Thompson's personal safety depended on the contents of the trunk being in safe hands, and asks Parker to keep it safe until "you shall hear from me or from my *Executors*." Clearly, it was time for Thompson to extricate himself from what was becoming an impossible situation, and he set about doing so in the methodical way that was becoming his trademark.

As a first step, he had sold some of the land inherited from his grandfather to Loammi Baldwin's older brother, Cyrus. The elder brother kept a shop in Boston, and in anticipation of his return to the town, Thompson agreed to accept payment in the form of goods. Then, in August he wrote a letter to his father-in-law, now in the archive of the New Hampshire Historical Society, carefully constructed to put his flight in the best possible light. He was, he said,

> *determined to seek for that Peace & Protection in foreign Lands, & among Strangers, which is deny'd me in my native Country. I cannot any longer bear the insults that are daily offered me. I cannot bear to be look'd upon & treated as the Achan of Society.[7] I have done nothing that can deserve this Cruel usage. I have done nothing with any desire to injure my Countrymen, & cannot any longer bear to be treated in this barbarous manner by them.*

As for his wife and daughter, he asks the minister to take care of them in their "distressed circumstances" that "call for every indulgence &

alleviation you can afford them." This isn't quite as callous as it sounds because his wife remained one of the richest women in the locality, but it certainly does not indicate that the marriage was a love match, at least on his side. This was almost certainly the last communication from Thompson received by his father-in-law, who died on September 2, 1782.

The actual trigger for Thompson's departure seems to have been the unmasking of Benjamin Church as a spy for the British and his arrest at the beginning of October. In a letter dated October 5,[8] Washington recorded that he had sent a man to seize Church's papers from his home, "but it appeared, on inquiry, that a confidant had been among the papers before my messenger arrived." Historians agree that the finger points to Thompson as that confidant, hastily retrieving documents that might incriminate him, and papers valuable to the British. And because Church himself might now be about to incriminate him, Thompson had to move quickly, taking those papers with him to General Gage.

On October 10, Thompson drew up "A State of Benja. Thompson's Affairs in the Province of Massachusetts,"[9] detailing his debts, creditors, and other financial matters to be settled. He told his half-brother, Josiah Pierce, that he was leaving for the West Indies, and three days later, in the evening of Friday, October 13, Pierce drove Thompson down to Narragansett Bay, to board his ship.[10] After the brothers had said their farewells, however, Thompson was picked up by a boat from the British frigate *Scarborough* and rowed out to the ship, which took him to Boston. Useful though Thompson had been to Gage, he was not a sufficiently important spy to justify sending a frigate to pick him up at this time of crisis, and the inference is that he was carrying Church's papers with valuable intelligence.

By a twist of fate, Church himself probably did end up in the West Indies. After being held in jail for more than a year, he was allowed to board a schooner heading for those islands in 1777. Nothing more is known of him. But plenty more is known about Benjamin Thompson.

When Thompson arrived in Boston, he reported to General William Howe, who had been brought out by the *Scarborough* to take over as commander in chief of the British forces, with the information we mentioned earlier. His friends and family, of course, had no idea where he was, or what he was doing, and made fruitless efforts to find out. We know where Thompson was at the end of 1775 and in the early months of 1776, but we have very little idea what he was doing while he was in Boston. Thompson later claimed that his time in Boston had largely been spent in raising a regiment of American loyalists, but he was always prone to exaggerating and embellishing his own history. A more reliable indication comes in a letter dated February 7, 1776, from Baldwin's wife to her husband, who was then with Washington's forces in Cambridge, referring to the storekeeper Cyrus Baldwin: "I must inform you that Brother Cyrus saw Mr. Parkman,—informs him that our famous Major Thompson is in Boston, a clerk for a Major—."

After a series of military setbacks, the British position in Boston became unsustainable, and Howe evacuated the city on March 17, 1776. The troops and well over a thousand loyalist evacuees went to Halifax, Nova Scotia. Judge William Brown was given the task of carrying the important dispatches reporting this disaster, and sailed for England. Somehow, Benjamin Thompson managed to make himself part of the judge's entourage. He arrived in London in the spring of 1776, and immediately set about finding an opportunity of advancement. He was just twenty-three.

Opinion in England was far from being solidly behind the war in America. Many ordinary people felt sympathy with the complaints of the colonists, and more eminent proponents of a swift and amicable settlement of their grievances included John Wilkes, Edmund Burke, and the former Prime Minister Lord Rockingham—Governor Wentworth's former mentor. But the prime minister since 1770 had been Lord North, who wanted the rebellion crushed by force, and the king, George III, wholeheartedly concurred. Their Secretary of State for the Colonies, in charge of the war, was Lord George Germain, whose career depended on quashing the rebellion. Naturally, Thompson presented himself to Germain as an expert on the political and military situation in New England, offering a recommendation from his friend the governor of New Hampshire and a letter from General Howe that could hardly have been more glowing:

Benjamin Thompson Esq. having been forced to abandon a compe-
tent state in the Province of New Hampshire, from whence he was
cruelly driven by persecution and severe Maltreatment, on account
of his Loyal & faithful Efforts to support the Laws and promote the
service of Government, took refuge in Boston, Where as well as in the
Country he has endeavour'd to be useful to His Majesty's service, and
is therefore to be considered as deserving of Protection & Favours.

And we can be sure that Germain was apprised of Thompson's role as a spy.

In the wake of the fall of Boston, and with vocal opposition to the war in London, Germain needed all the help he could get, and Thompson must have seemed like a godsend. He was immediately appointed as Germain's private secretary, and the up-to-date inside knowledge he provided of conditions in Boston enabled Germain to give a rather undeserved impression of competence to the House of Commons, and keep his job.

PART II

A Servant of the Crown

CHAPTER 3

Civil Service

UNTIL HE INHERITED HIS PRESENT TITLE IN 1770, GERMAIN HAD BEEN known as Lord George Sackville; he was born in 1716 as the third son of Lionel Sackville, the first Duke of Dorset. Under that name, he had had a military career that started out promisingly but ended in disgrace. By 1759, during the Seven Years' War, Sackville had become the commander of the British troops fighting the French on the continent, but under the overall command of the Hanoverian Duke of Brunswick. At the Battle of Minden, on August 1, 1759, the combined British and Hanoverian infantry repulsed an attack by French cavalry and forced them to fall back. The duke repeatedly sent orders to Sackville for a cavalry charge to follow up this success, but Sackville refused to send his cavalry after the retreating French because he had a personal grudge against the commander of the cavalry, Lord Granby, and did not want him to receive the glory of success. Hardly surprisingly, Sackville was sacked and recalled to England; rubbing salt into the wound, he was replaced as commander of the British forces by Granby.

In an act of arrogant stupidity, Sackville now demanded a court martial in order to clear his name from accusations of cowardice. In 1760 the court not only found him guilty but concluded that he was "unfit to serve His Majesty in any military Capacity whatever" and ordered that this damning verdict should be entered in the orderly book of every regiment in the army. Contemporaries described this disgrace as "worse than death." But it seems to have been no bar to a political career, at a time when being an MP depended simply on who you were and how much money you had. Luck also played a part in Sackville's rehabilitation. The indecisive conclusion to the Seven Years' War encouraged official amnesia about its less glorious aspects, and the accession of George III later in 1760 marked a new beginning. His predecessor, George II, had been pro-German and pro the Seven Years' War; his grandson, George III, hated his grandfather and everything he stood for, and Sackville, playing the long game, had positioned himself in the grandson's camp. By 1769, when Sackville inherited the title Lord Germain and the estates that went with it, he was a prominent supporter of Lord North and received appropriate patronage when North became prime minister. Germain, as he now was, was still arrogant and self-serving (and not too bright), but that was par for the course in those days, and in November 1775 he became Secretary of State for the American Department. His commission read in part that he was appointed "for the restoration of public tranquillity among his Majesty's deluded subjects in the affected colonies." In that capacity, he was in fact one of the key architects of the disastrous British response to the unrest in the North American colonies.

Thompson's arrival in London in April 1776, armed with glowing testimonials, a reputation as an expert on the situation in America, and secretly known as a successful British spy, must have seemed like a godsend to Germain, at a time when the government still hoped that the fall of Boston was a temporary setback and that the war in America might still be won. Germain immediately appointed Thompson as one of his private secretaries, and armed with Thompson's local knowledge he was able to present himself as an expert on the situation in New England. Thompson's reward was not long coming. On December 15, 1776, Germain petitioned the king with the request that "the Loyalty, Integrity, and Ability of Our Trusty and Welbeloved Benjamin Thompson" should be recognized by appointing him as Secretary and Register of Records for the Province of Georgia. Given the situation in America—the Declaration of Independence had been made in July that year—this was a largely meaningless position, but the king was happy to make the appointment, and Thompson, still only twenty-three, was happy to accept it, with the £100 per annum that went with the job. Ellis, who knew nothing of

Thompson's activities as a spy, nevertheless astutely points out that "he must have said or done something at once to secure his ready welcome."

At this point in our story, Thompson goes off the radar. For the next few years, there is no paper trail to account for what he was doing on Germain's behalf. But this is no surprise given the way Germain worked. He had always been an unpleasant piece of work, but following his rise, fall, and rise again he had become even more vindictive and manipulative, using every trick he could to destroy the reputation of his opponents. He had his own network of spies throughout the government and the army, which consumed a budget of around £3,000 a year from his inherited wealth. It is easy to see how Thompson would have fitted into Germain's entourage, and equally easy to see why no record of what he was doing survives. What little we know about Thompson for the years between 1776 and 1779 comes from secondhand hearsay and gossip, although that is quite revealing.

What evidence there is has been gathered and pieced together by Sanborn Brown. In his diary, written in 1801, Lord Glenbervie records[1] that

> *Lady Glenbervie remembers [Thompson] going about with Lady George [Germain] and her daughters to balls as a sort of humble dependent and dancing with the young ladies when they could get no other partner. At that time he was considered as the favourite, at once, of the father, mother and daughters, and the ill-fame of the father then, and the conduct of the daughters since, have served to keep the scandal alive with regard to them.*

The balls Thompson attended were not just in London, but also in fashionable Bath, an image, like that of his carriage in Concord, familiar from Jane Austen. The "ill-fame of the father then" is a reference to something not so familiar from Austen's novels—the widespread gossip and insinuation that Lord George Germain was a practicing homosexual, an accusation that had been flung at him as far back as the time of his disgrace after Minden. Glenbervie's diary entry is not the only time that Thompson's name is linked with that of Germain in this context, and as

Brown puts it, "This should be born in mind when we see . . . the tremendous hold that Thompson had on Lord George when he needed favors done for himself." As we shall see, Thompson certainly had an eye for the ladies; but he also had an eye for the main chance, and Germain clearly offered his best chance of a successful career in England. Another refugee, Samuel Curwen, who had formerly been Deputy Judge of Admiralty in Salem, refers to him as having "breakfast, dinner and supper" with Lord George, "so great a favourite is he."[2]

Thompson emerges from the shadows in 1779, when he is acting as the point of contact for American refugees in London seeking the help of Germain. To anyone familiar with Samuel Pepys's diary, there are echoes in his behavior in this role of the way Pepys handled supplicants in his capacity as naval administrator a century earlier. The refugees were not, initially, penniless. They were largely respectable professionals and landowners, with their families, who had come to England to ride out the storm, ready to return home to America when the British army had restored order. It only slowly dawned on them, as their funds began to run out, that this was not going to happen, and meanwhile they formed a community of exiles who clung together and did not—unlike Thompson, who had thoroughly burned his boats—try to make their own way in England. When the penny began to drop, they felt that their loyalty ought to be recognized by receiving recompense and financial support from the government. Grants made to the refugees for the losses they had incurred "back home" ran into the tens of thousands of pounds per year; but the government blamed them for not keeping their own house in order in the colonies, and only grudgingly paid out £100 a year to keep anyone who could not prove a serious loss—the vast majority—from destitution. If they wanted more help, financial or otherwise, the man they had to deal with was Thompson. As poacher turned gamekeeper, he was far from sympathetic to their plight.

One, possibly extreme, example is known from the diaries of a doctor and apothecary, John Jeffries, which are now housed in the archive of the Houghton Library of Harvard University. Jeffries was one of the exiles who had fled initially to Halifax, where he found a good hospital job, but could not be paid until the appointment had been confirmed by the authorities in London. With no sign of the necessary paperwork, Jeffries went to London with his wife Sarah (known as Susan) to try to get things sorted out. They arrived on April 2, 1779, and were introduced to Thompson, described in the diary as "the present Favourite of Lord Germain," who promised that he would "inform him [Germain] fully" of Jeffries's situation. While Johnson was getting the runaround from officialdom in London over the next few weeks, Thompson was having his own runaround with Mrs. Jeffries, whose husband, willing to put up with anything, it seems, in order to get his affairs sorted, records the many occasions on which "Mrs J" spent the night with "Mr Thompson of Pall Mall." Thompson also took Susan out on the town, including visits to Sadler's Wells and to the Vauxhall Pleasure Gardens on the south side of the River Thames. When eventually Jeffries's commission as apothecary was approved, he was told that as he had left Halifax without permission he was in London illegally and that he must leave at once without asking any further favors. He sailed for New York (still in British hands) in July, leaving behind in Thompson's care some documents that Thompson promptly appropriated for his own benefit.

The papers were a collection of political letters by Benjamin Franklin and a governor of Massachusetts, Thomas Pounall, to and from an activist, a Reverend Cooper. They gave an insight into political developments in America between 1769 and 1774. Cooper had left Boston in a hurry during Gage's time in charge and gave the letters for safekeeping to a fellow sympathizer to the cause. That sympathizer happened to be the father of John Jeffries. John, who did not share his father's politics, got hold of the documents, and took them to London with him. In his diary, Jeffries says that on June 14, 1779, he gave Thompson the letters "for inspection." Thompson took them away and never brought them back. Instead, with Jeffries on the other side of the ocean, he had the letters bound in red morocco and presented them to the king "as a literary as well as a political curiosity."

As well as providing an insight into Thompson's character, however, his interaction with Jeffries puts us back on the track of his development as a scientist. Jeffries was a keen amateur natural philosopher,[3] and his diary entry of April 28, 1779, records a "long conversation with

[Thompson] upon Speculative Philosophy." This was just at the time Thompson was involved in experiments that led to the publication of his first scientific paper, on the explosive force of gunpowder.

This was a natural topic for investigation at a time when Britain was almost constantly at war but gunnery was as much an art as a science. No two cannon were the same, cannonballs themselves were only roughly standardized, and the amount of gunpowder used in firing the cannon, and its exact composition, varied. There was a popular myth among gunners at the time that the range of their cannon was increased when they used damp gunpowder, the "explanation" being that steam produced in the explosion of the powder added to the impetus given to the ball. We now know that the argument fails because heat is used up converting the water into steam, so the gases are not as hot if damp gunpowder is used. But as we shall see, the nature of heat was still a mystery in the 1770s. In the spring of 1778, Germain and a group of friends including Thompson had been arguing about this at Germain's estate, in what is now East Sussex. It was Thompson who decided to settle the argument by carrying out a series of experiments—testing the hypothesis that damp gunpowder is more effective in the proper scientific manner, rather than just arguing about it.

His first experiment was disarmingly simple, but used the now classic scientific technique of eliminating all possible variables and making the tests reproducible. He took a carefully measured amount of gunpowder mixed with a carefully measured small amount of water and used it to prime a pistol that lay on the ground pointing at an oak plank. The pistol was fired using a trail of gunpowder, and he measured both the distance the ball penetrated into the wood and the distance that the pistol recoiled. Always using powder from the same barrel, he repeated the experiment with different amounts of water. He found that the explosive force was always less with added water, and the more water he added the less the force. For good measure he also tried mixing in alcohol, turpentine, and even mercury. Nothing was as effective as dry gunpowder alone.

These rather ad hoc experiments roused considerable interest in London, and Thompson got Germain's permission to go back to his estate, then known as Stoneland Lodge but now Buckhurst Park, to carry out a longer series of more precise tests using a small cannon. In all, he spent nine days carrying out twenty-three experiments to measure just about everything he could along these lines. In the 1770s, a device called a ballistic pendulum was used to measure the speed of projectiles fired from a gun. This was basically a large block of suspended wood. When a bullet was fired into the wood, it would recoil, and the amount by which the pendulum swung could be used to calculate the force imparted by the bullet—essentially the same technique is still used today. It's a straightforward application of Newton's laws of motion, but to put this in perspective, in the 1770s Newton's laws had been known for less than a century. Thompson realized that a lot of the force of the gunpowder was dissipated in the hot gases expelled by the gun, so he devised an improved pendulum technique in which the gun was also suspended, and the amount by which it recoiled when it was fired was measured. This gave a direct measurement of the total amount of force exerted by the gunpowder in the opposite direction. The basic setup involved firing the cannon (actually just the barrel), suspended on a pendulum, at a heavy target, also suspended on a pendulum, and measuring how far each pendulum swung.

The main conclusion from the series of experiments was indeed that dry gunpowder is the most effective, and along the way he showed how to determine the quality of the powder from these measurements. He also investigated such details as the best position for the vent hole of the gun. But something extra, carried out almost as an afterthought, turned out to indicate a much deeper insight, although this was not understood at the time. Thompson, who, as he often tells us, had been fascinated by the nature of heat since childhood, noticed that when he touched the barrel of the cannon immediately after it had been fired, it was hotter after it had been fired with a blank charge, with no ball in the barrel. He had expected that the barrel would be hotter if it had been loaded, because the ball would have confined the heat of the exploding powder in the barrel far longer. But he consistently found that the barrel actually became hotter when the gun was firing blanks. His tentative conclusion was that the heating of the barrel was due to a sudden expansion and contraction of the barrel; he wrote, "It being pretty evident that [the heat] is not all communicated by the flame, there is but one other cause to which it can be attributed, and that is the motion and friction of the internal parts of the metal among themselves, occasioned by the sudden and violent effort of the powder upon the inside of the bore." This is not entirely correct, because Thompson did not appreciate that energy is carried away by the cannonball when the gun is loaded. But it is his first recorded suggestion that heat is produced by motion.

Thompson's paper, ninety-nine pages long, was published in the *Philosophical Transactions* of the Royal Society on January 1, 1781, under the splendid title "New Experiments upon Gun-powder, with Occasional Observations and Practical Inferences; to Which Are Added, an Account of a New Method of Determining the Velocity of All Kinds of Military Projectiles, and the Description of a Very Accurate Eprouvette for Gun-powder." It had already been formally read to the society and earned him election as a Fellow of the Royal Society in April 1779, a month after his twenty-sixth birthday. This was the same year that Joseph Banks[4] was elected as the president of the society; he would soon become, in all but name, the scientific adviser to the British government. One of Thompson's proposers for election as a Fellow was Daniel Solander, a naturalist who had sailed with Banks on Cook's first circumnavigation of the globe; the citation described Thompson as "Benjamin Thompson Esq, of Concord in the Province of New Hampshire in New England. A Gentleman well versed in natural Knowledge and in many Branches of Polite Learning." The new Fellow became an active member of the society, regularly attending its meetings when he was in London, contributing to the discussions there, and becoming a friend of Banks. Thompson's new status as a gunnery expert also led to his next adventure, although in line with Germain's devious methods the gunnery seems chiefly to have been a cover for skullduggery.

In 1775, when Germain had been appointed Secretary of State for the Colonies, the British still expected to be able to crush fairly swiftly the rebellion in America. The situation changed dramatically in the middle of 1778, when France declared war on Britain (ostensibly in support of the Americans, but the French were always ready for an excuse to declare war on Britain), with Spain following suit in 1779. Germain saw this as an opportunity to extend his power base, and with the approval of the king, George III, became minister of war in all but name, in overall charge of army operations. Even this wasn't enough for him, and he tried to take control of the navy as well, on the not entirely specious grounds that the situation on the other side of the Atlantic required close cooperation between the forces on land and on sea. This brought him into bitter conflict with the First Lord of the Admiralty, the Earl of Sandwich, exactly at the time Thompson was making a name for himself as an expert on gunnery.[5] What could be more natural than that Germain's favorite, and secret informer, should volunteer to go to sea with the fleet to carry out experiments in naval gunnery and suggest how it might be improved? With, of course, the confidential brief to find out anything he could that would enable Germain to dish the dirt on Sandwich and his control of the navy.

There was, in truth, plenty of dirt to dish. At this critical time, the royal navy was badly equipped, badly supplied, and badly managed both from Whitehall and by senior officers at sea. Thompson sailed in 1779 with Admiral Sir Charles Hardy, who was in command of the Channel Fleet. This was a key command in any war with continental powers, especially France, but Hardy was an elderly man called out of retirement to take on the job because of political intrigues that had led to the dismissal and disgrace of a predecessor and a consequent reluctance among serving officers to take on the task. Thompson provided Germain with exactly the information he wanted, writing long (and at the time, secret) letters detailing the deficiencies with the fleet. His conclusion was that brave men were being let down by stupid and incompetent commanders, and in a typical comment he wrote, "I call God and Heaven to witness that it gives me pain when I tell you that I think Sir Charles Hardy is not a fit person to command this great fleet."

One of the deficiencies Thompson pounced on concerned the inadequacies of the system of flags used to signal between ships. This was actually a well-known problem, and being actively investigated by several naval experts, including Captain Richard Kempenfelt, who commanded Hardy's flagship, the *Victory*.[6] It was Kempenfelt's system of codes for specific maneuvers represented by numbers indicated by flags that was adopted and became the standard in the turbulent decades that followed. Thompson's restless inventiveness led him also to invent a new system of flag signaling, although it was never adopted and the details have been lost. One reference to this comes from the diary of Samuel Curwen, highlighting the remarkable rise of the shop assistant he had once known:

> *This young man, when a shop-lad to my next neighbor, ever appeared active, good-natured, and sensible; by a strange concurrence of events, he is now Under-Secretary to the American Secretary of State, Lord George Germain, a secretary to Georgia, inspector of all the clothing sent to America. . . . His income arising from these sources is, I have been told, near seven thousand[7] a year—a sum infinitely beyond his most sanguine expectations. He is, besides, a member of the Royal Society. It is said he is of an ingenious turn, and inventive imagination and, by being on a cruise in Channel Service with Sir Charles Hardy, has formed a more regular and better-digested system for signals than that heretofore used. He seems to be of a happy, even temper in general deportment.*

But one thing Thompson certainly was not doing while with the Channel Fleet was carrying out any significant experiments with gunpowder and guns. Thompson was always eager to promote his own work at length and publish his results in detail—as with his gunpowder paper in the *Philosophical Transactions*. He would go into extensive (even obsessive) detail about what he had done. But the only mention of any studies carried out while he was at sea came in a paper summarizing his work on gunpowder that he published in 1797 and can be found in the *Collected Works*. Almost as an aside, he mentions that "during a cruise which I made, as a volunteer in the 'Victory,' with the British fleet, under the command of my late worthy friend Sir Charles Hardy" he had observed the distances at which cannon balls fell into the sea when fired from the heavy guns during exercises, which gave him "opportunities of making several very interesting experiments, which gave me much new light relative to the action of fired gunpowder." This suggests that while he observed the gunnery in action during practice drills,[8] he did not carry out any experiments like those he had performed at Stoneland Lodge. He seems to have been much more interested, during his three months with the fleet, in the science of sailing and the design of ships. So much so that back on dry land he not only studied naval architecture but came up with his own design for an improved large forty-gun frigate with a crew of 250, and tried to persuade the admiralty to build a ship to his design. His efforts were unsuccessful, even though Captain Kempenfelt wrote a letter in support of his application, but the detailed plans for his design survive, and modern experts agree that it would probably have been a fast and successful addition to the royal navy.

Any thoughts of a career in naval architecture, however, disappeared when Germain found a way to reward Thompson for his loyal, but mostly undercover, service over the past four years. Thompson was back ashore in the autumn of 1779, and soon afterward Germain appointed him as deputy to the inspector general of provincial forces. Unlike the post of secretary and register of records for the Province of Georgia, this was a real job with real responsibilities. But with those responsibilities came the opportunity to get rich, entirely within the bounds of acceptable behavior of the day.

Thompson's work, as mentioned in Curwen's diary, involved supplying all the clothing and equipment sent from England to the forces serving in America. Because his superior, the inspector general, was based in Charleston, South Carolina, he had a completely free hand in London. Instead of officials such as Thompson acting as government agents when purchasing goods, buying them directly from a supplier with government funds, the way things were done in Thompson's day was for the official in charge to buy the goods as cheaply as possible using his own money, then to sell them to the government (or in this case the army) at as high a price as he could obtain, and pocket the difference. This was completely standard practice, and anyone who did not profit from a position like the one now held by Thompson was regarded as a fool. Clearly Germain had this in mind when he rewarded his loyal spy with the appointment. But Thompson's scientific curiosity, combined with an unscrupulous adherence to the accepted practice, enabled him to profit even more than Germain may have anticipated.

In January 1781[9] Thompson carried out experiments to measure the "Specific Gravity, Diameter, Strength, Cohesion etc. of Silk," an important material used in the manufacture of uniforms. He found it very difficult to get consistent results from these experiments, because of the way they were affected by the amount of moisture the silk contained. In order to remove this variable from the equations, he dried the silk threads by a fire, and he noted that

> *Silk possesses a power of attracting and imbibing water from the air. . . . [I]t appears that a Merchant or manufacturer who purchases 100 lbs of raw silk, in a common state as to dryness actually pays for at least 8 lbs of Water, and if it has been Kept for any considerable time in a place the quantity of moisture imbibed will be still greater.*

It would be naive to think that Thompson did not take advantage of this knowledge in his role as deputy to the inspector general of provincial forces. Simply by buying silk by weight in the driest state he could find, then sending it on a long, damp sea voyage to Charleston or New York, where he sold it by weight to the army, he could make a considerable profit, over and above the markup he received on the price per pound weight, in effect by selling water to them. And there was nothing illegal, nor even (by the standards of the day) immoral about any of this.

Although he took the usual personal advantage from his position, Thompson was, however, also diligent about getting the supplies they needed to the troops, and went further by getting bayonets added to the long guns (known as fusees) of the horse guards for use when fighting on foot.

Alongside his new work, Thompson continued to act as the conduit for loyalist refugees seeking help from Germain. And he continued to be unsympathetic to their pleas, now seeing himself as an English gentleman whose future lay in London, and trying to put his past behind him. His process of assimilation into the British establishment continued in September 1780, when one of the two undersecretaries of state in Germain's office resigned to concentrate on other work, and Thompson was appointed in his place; he first signed papers in his new capacity on October 27. He was now responsible for arranging the transport of troops and supplies (including weapons) to the other side of the Atlantic, and involved in discussions about the defense of Caribbean islands, trade with the islands off Central America, and other weighty matters. This was serious political business, even if he was number two to Germain. The snag was, as we shall see, that he was so closely associated with Germain that if and when Lord George fell from favor he would take Thompson down with him.

The first signs of this fall came in the very month, September 1780, that Thompson was appointed as undersecretary. The situation in America was deteriorating, and public sentiment was turning against the war, not least because of the high taxation required to pay not just for the forces in America but for defense against the continental powers allied to the rebels. The government, dominated by Lord North, the Earl of Sandwich, and Germain, was so unpopular that the king dissolved Parliament and there was a general election in November. The result was that the North administration remained in power, but with a majority in Parliament cut to just six. It staggered on, but increasingly had to make concessions to the opposition. By January 1782, Germain was out of office. He was used as something of a scapegoat, carrying the can for the failures of the administration, but as so often happens in such circumstances, he was gotten rid of by being promoted; in February 1782 he was made Baron Bolebrooke, in the County of Sussex, and Viscount Sackville, of Drayton in the County of Northampton. Not bad for a failure. But by then, Thompson, having seen which way the wind was blowing, and perhaps prompted by another potential threat, had made good his escape—initially, and bizarrely, back to America.

CHAPTER 4

Military Service

THOMPSON'S PLAN WAS TO REINVENT HIMSELF AS A MILITARY MAN. THIS was easy to do in those days, provided you were a gentleman and had enough money. The fact that Thompson really did have a modest background in the military was a bonus, but unnecessary. In order to reduce costs to the exchequer, private individuals with an appropriate standing in society and plenty of money were allowed to raise regiments at their own expense and provide them to the army, if they could find a general willing to take the regiment under his wing. There was even an official handbook that listed the cost of purchasing a commission with a particular rank. It was an expensive and risky business (in more ways than one), but tempting to someone in Thompson's position. He would, of course, have a high rank in his own regiment, as lieutenant colonel; and when the unit was disbanded at the end of hostilities, like other officers he would not only keep the rank in civilian life but receive half the pay of a serving officer with the same rank until he died.

This arrangement was, as far as the provincial forces were concerned, a new one that was of key interest to Thompson, and that he knew all about because it originated from a decision made by Germain at the beginning of 1779. Before that time, only officers in the regular British army qualified, and while on active service their orders superseded the orders of the local men, even when the locals were nominally the superior in rank. Germain decided to encourage recruitment and enthusiasm among the loyalist Americans by abolishing the distinction. On January

23, 1769, he wrote to Sir Henry Clinton, the overall commander of British forces in America, that

> *It is . . . his Majesty's pleasure that you publish and make known to his provincial corps, as also to all others his loyal subjects in America, his gracious intention to support and protect them by making the rank of the officers permanent in America, and allowing them half-pay upon the reduction of their regiments, in the same manner as the officers of British reduced regiments are paid.*

Whatever the effect on the loyalists, the decision to recognize their ranks in this way upset the British regulars, and did nothing to encourage smooth cooperation between them and the provincial forces. It was against this background that in 1780 a Captain Daniel Murray offered to raise a force of light dragoons in America, to be commanded by Brigadier Timothy Ruggles, a loyalist who had had high command in the French and Indian Wars. Responding to this suggestion, on June 7, 1780, Germain wrote to Clinton:

> *The services of Brigadier Ruggles in the last war, and the influence he still retains in those provinces of North America, where his character, his honour, and his name are respected, made me long desirous of seeing that gentleman engaged in the King's service. The enclosed plan of raising a regiment of dragoons was communicated to me by Captain Murray, by authority of Brigadier Ruggles. It appeared to me so fair and so disinterested, that I laid it before his Majesty, and it so far met with his royal approbation that he permitted me to transmit the plan to you. And if the public service requires any provincial cavalry to be raised, his Majesty would be pleased to see Mr. Ruggles placed at the head of such a corps, where he may have an opportunity of again acting with that zeal and spirit which formerly did him so much honour.*

Clinton vetoed the scheme, on the grounds that the "new" cavalry unit would be partly staffed by officers recruited from existing units, who could not afford to lose them. But Thompson, who was privy to all the toing and froing of correspondence involved, had meanwhile come up with his own plan to raise a cavalry unit entirely from loyalists who were not yet in the armed forces, and at his own expense. We don't know exactly when Thompson first hatched this plan, but John Jeffries, now back in New York, records in his diary in October 1780 how he was sounding out loyalists who later became officers in the new unit.

Thompson probably had no intention, initially, of leading his regiment into battle. In spite of his rank, he could have stayed in London and reaped the rewards of his investment without actually getting involved in the shooting war. He obtained permission to recruit an outfit in New York to be called the King's American Dragoons, and he persuaded Murray, who was in London at the time, to go back to America to recruit soldiers for the regiment. His commission as lieutenant colonel, obtained in February 1781, alone cost him £4,500, a clear indication of how wealthy he had become, and he also provided Murray with funds to provide a bounty to new recruits. In the summer of 1782, when recruitment was being completed, an advertisement Thompson placed in *Rivington's Royal Gazette* offered 10 guineas to any "likely and spirited young lads" who "prefer riding on horseback to going on foot," and 5 guineas to any recruit who persuaded another man to join, plus 5 guineas to the second man. The fact that this was the highest bounty offered by any loyalist regiment raised during the war allowed it to recruit its full establishment even after the surrender of Lord Cornwallis and his army to combined French and American forces at Yorktown, Virginia, on October 19, 1781—the turning point of the war. Until that point, it had seemed that the southern provinces, at least, might still be held by the British. But by the time news of that battle reached London, Thompson was on his way to New York to take personal command of his cavalry, having hurriedly wound up his affairs in London. On September 28 Thompson's successor as undersecretary[1] wrote to the admiralty:[2]

I am directed by Lord George Germain to desire you would move the Lords Commissioners of the Admiralty to give the necessary Orders, that Lieutenant Colonel Thompson who is going out to serve in His Majesty's Provincial Forces in America, may be received on board the

Rotterdam or any other of His Majesty's Ships of war appointed to Convoy the Fleet preparing to sail for New York.

And on September 30 Germain himself wrote to Clinton:[3]

I beg leave to introduce Mr. Thompson to you, and at the same time to thank you for the favour and protection which you have shewn him in giving him the command of a regiment of light dragoons, which, I trust, will be raised in a manner to entitle the officers of it to your approbation. Lieutenant-Colonel Thompson shows at least a spirit and zeal for the service, in quitting for a time an agreeable and profitable civil situation, in the hopes of being useful to his country, and by his military conduct, shewing himself not unworthy of the protection which you have granted him. If you do him the honour to converse with him, you will find him well informed, and, as far as theory goes, a good officer in whatever you may think fit to employ him. I can answer for his honour and his ability, and I am persuaded he will ever feel himself attached by gratitude to you for the very kind and obliging manner in which you have protected him and the regiment under his command.

Germain, of course, knew as well as we do that the writing was on the wall as far as Thompson's "agreeable and profitable civil situation" was concerned, but he was hardly going to tell Clinton that! He probably knew better than we do what prompted Thompson to up sticks and leave England in something of a hurry. Nobody can now be sure what prompted the sudden move, but as well as Germain's clearly imminent fall from grace, with its inevitable repercussions for his favorite, there was a spy scandal at the time to which Thompson's name (among others, it should be said) was linked.

Early in 1781, a French spy ring headed by Francis Henry de la Motte that had been passing information about the royal navy was unmasked. La Motte was brought to trial on July 23 and found guilty. One of his accomplices, a man called Lutterloh, turned king's evidence and confessed in exchange for a lighter sentence; la Motte himself was "dragged on a hurdle" to Tyburn, the notorious place of execution near the present-day site of Marble Arch, where he was hanged and quartered. But there was a third member of the spy ring, an informer identified only as "a Friend in a certain office." This highly publicized scandal led to a great deal of speculation about the identity of the third man, who had to be someone with powerful friends able to protect him from investigation. Thompson's name was one of those bandied about by the gossips in this regard. The rumors never really died. Much later, when (as we discuss in chapter 7) Thompson (by then Count Rumford) was a candidate to run the US Military Academy, the then American ambassador in London, Rufus King, was asked to check up on his background. King recorded in his memorandum book, although not in any official communiqué back to Washington, that it was accepted in informed circles "that R[umford] was connected with La Motte the French spy" and that Germain

> learning that Lord Sandwich was about to bring R. to trial, sent him [Sandwich] a message at the time that the motion was before Parliament to address the King to remove from his confidence, etc. Lord Sandwich, that if he persisted in his intentions about R., he Ld. Geo. with all his friends would vote for the motion, wh[ich] would have carried it. . . . [T]his protection proceeded from the scandalous intimacy between Ld. George and R.[4]

In other words, at least some people in high places believed that Thompson had been providing information to the French, presumably for money, and that he was in a homosexual relationship with Germain that enabled him to blackmail Germain into twisting the arm of Sandwich. The fact that the story is plausible, if unproven, tells us a lot about both Germain and Thompson (and the politics of late eighteenth-century Britain), and could certainly explain why Thompson wanted to get out of England for a while. He left late in October 1781, and knew he was sailing into trouble, not just from the rebel forces. In spite of Germain's flowery prose in his letter to Clinton, there was no love lost between Lord George and Sir Henry, and Thompson must have been aware that Clinton would treat any protégé of Germain with suspicion, if not hostility.

Indeed, his initial reception in America suggests a deliberate campaign of harassment, which can only have been instigated by Clinton. But what started out as an unfortunate landfall in America turned out to provide him with an opportunity to make a name for himself and rise in the estimation of the generals, and even of Sir Henry himself.

The voyage itself provided an opportunity for Thompson to carry out more gunnery experiments. He tells us in his 1897 paper on gunpowder,

> *His Majesty having been graciously pleased to permit me to take out with me from England four pieces of light artillery, constructed under the direction of the late Lieutenant-General Desaguliers, with a large proportion of ammunition, I made a great number of interesting experiments with these guns, and also with the ship's guns on board the ships of war in which I made my passage to and from America.*

The guns and ammunition were a gift of the king, showing that Thompson was still in favor at court, whatever political machinations were going on in Parliament.

When Thompson left England, it was still possible for people there to hope for a British victory in the American war; by the time he landed in America, late in December, the war was effectively lost—news of the Yorktown disaster reached Germain on November 25. Thompson's personal predicament also looked bleak. Instead of arriving in New York where his regiment was being raised, Thompson landed at Charleston,[5] in Carolina, where the convoy had been blown by uncooperative winds. He was in the wrong place, at the wrong time. But being who he was, Thompson made the most of his situation. In the process, he turned out to be rather good at a certain kind of soldiering; we shouldn't really be surprised at this, as he generally turned out to be rather good at anything he turned his hand to.

What may have been a program of deliberate harassment—or perhaps simply a result of incompetence—began almost as soon as Thompson was safely ashore. He had with him the usual paraphernalia of a traveling officer, including servants and his horses, plus the four guns given to him by the king. It took the best part of a day to get everything on to dry land, at which point Thompson was told that the *Rotterdam* was to sail almost immediately for New York. Once everything was back on board, he was told that this had been a mistake, and he should unload again. Next day, with all Thompson's gear back on land, the ship sailed without him, leaving the convoy to spend the winter in harbor. The most likely explanation of these shenanigans is that while the unloading and reloading was going on the commander in Charleston, General Alexander Leslie, received word from Clinton to delay Thompson's arrival in New York. As Thompson wrote to Germain, "I find I shall stand in need of all my prudence to steer clear of all the snares and lures that will surround me."[6] He also wrote:

> *My being left behind, and the Rotterdam's sailing for New York, as she did, without my knowledge, I am convinced was not without design, and management.*

With nothing else to do in Charleston, Thompson asked Leslie for an active role, and was given the title "Commandant de la Cavalerie" and put in charge of a rather mixed group of about two hundred horsemen and five hundred foot soldiers, with a couple of guns. It is unlikely that Leslie expected much to come of this except to keep Thompson out of his hair, but he soon wrote approvingly to Clinton:[7]

> *The several detached corps of cavalry have been incorporated into distinct ones under the command of Lieutenant-Colonel Thompson. From the unwearied attention and diligent efforts of that officer they are become respectable, and I have everything to expect from this improvement.*

His expectations were soon fulfilled. The region occupied by the British was essentially under siege from the land side, morale was low after the loss of Yorktown, and the activity of the army was largely limited to sending out raiding parties to bring back food. On the other side, the Americans were now confident of victory, were well supplied, and with little action were becoming complacent, looking forward to the inevitable conclusion of the war in their favor. On both sides, men were waiting for hostilities to end so they could go home. Thompson, unlike many of his compatriots, was eager for action of any kind to enhance his reputation, and after bringing his forces up to scratch cut his teeth leading raiding parties. Then came an opportunity for something more dramatic.

In the last week of February 1782, Thompson took a large raiding party some forty miles north of Charleston, seizing a large number of cattle and other livestock to feed the garrison. Although American scouts reported the activity of this large body of men to their commander, General Francis Marion, and his deputy, Colonel Hezekiah Maham, these officers regarded it as just another hit-and-run raid, not expecting any real aggression from the British. Maham went home to look after his farm, and Marion went to bed, belying the nickname of "Swamp Fox" that he had earned through his skill at guerrilla warfare. But Thompson was actually looking for action, and meeting no opposition swept down on Marion's regiment on Sunday, February 24. The commander in the field, whose name (perhaps happily) is not recorded, was eating his Sunday lunch and ignored warnings from his scouts. When Thompson's cavalry charged into the camp, he belatedly leapt into action and was promptly killed. As the Americans scattered, forty of them died and Thompson took four prisoners.

With Maham still away, Marion took personal charge of the regiment, rallied his troops, and chased after Thompson as he headed back to Charleston. There was a further indecisive action in which twenty Americans were killed and sixteen prisoners taken, together with twenty muskets and "canteens full of liquor," according to Thompson's official report; Thompson lost only one man killed. He also took more than thirty horses and collected a large number of cattle on this expedition. With the benefit of hindsight, military historians have suggested that Thompson might have achieved even more if he had had a little more experience in the field, but this was nevertheless a rare, morale-boosting local victory for the British at a time when nothing else seemed to be going their way. If he had not done so already, Leslie now realized that Thompson was persona non grata with Clinton only for political reasons, and was fulsome in his praise of the lieutenant colonel's soldiering ability, writing in *Rivington's Royal Gazette* on March 1:

> *Lieutenant-General Leslie desires Lieutenant-Colonel Thompson and the officers and soldiers of the cavalry and infantry who served under his command will accept his best thanks for the services performed by them on the late expedition. The Lieutenant-General cannot too truly express to the army the opinion he entertains of the merit of Lieutenant-Colonel Thompson's conduct upon the occasion, and of the spirited behaviour of the troops. The constancy with which they supported the fatigues of a long and very rapid march claims his approbation, no less than their exertions in presence of the enemy.*

And to Clinton on March 12, 1782, that[8]

> *I had the honour to inform your Excellency that Lieutenant-Colonel Thompson having offered his service during his stay here, I had appointed him to the command of the cavalry. He has put them in exceeding good order and gained their confidence and affection. I am very happy to inform your Excellency of his success in a late excursion upon the Santee. I enclose to your Excellency Colonel Thompson's report to me of this very handsome piece of service, and I assure your Excellency that I have much regret to part with this enterprising young officer, who appears to have an uncommon share of merit and zeal for the service; and could he and his corps be spared to act in this part, where cavalry are so much wanted, I am confident it would tend much to the benefit of his Majesty's service.*

Thompson arrived in New York on April 11, 1782, hot on the heels of this letter. Thanks to the contrary winds that had forced him to winter in Charleston, he did not arrive as a gentleman amateur playing at soldiering and as a tool of Lord Germain. Germain had now gone from office, and Thompson was now an established cavalry officer, only just twenty-nine, seen as a rising star in the army. In any case, Clinton, blamed as overall commander at the time for the loss of Yorktown, had resigned, and was replaced as commander in chief by General Sir Guy Carleton, who had distinguished himself in the defense of Canada against the rebel American forces. Carleton had no reason to be hostile to Thompson, and every reason to welcome this proven cavalry officer and his regiment, if Thompson could complete his recruitment before the war ended. It was just the kind of new beginning Thompson must have hoped for when he left London, and although recruitment was no easy matter, it involved just the kind of organizational skills that Thompson excelled in.

The rules for raising a regiment were strict, and designed to minimize the cost to the Treasury, which maximized the financial risk to the officer funding the exercise. Until half of the required number of private soldiers had enlisted, the government made no financial contribution at all, but the men had to be paid. Once this magic number was reached, the government chipped in half-pay until the full complement was achieved, and only then took full responsibility for the payroll, including the officers. If the scheme failed, everything Thompson had paid out would be lost. In New York, there were further stipulations relevant to the officers recruited. They had to be loyalists who had suffered losses as a result of their commitment to the British cause, and who would give up any claim for compensation in return for the half-pay for life that they could expect when the regiment was disbanded. Thompson's indispensable aide in achieving all this, and setting up the organization of the regiment, was Daniel Murray, now promoted to major, who had been in New York for months working on Thompson's behalf.

Any suggestion that Thompson's regiment would not be officered by poaching men from existing units had been quietly forgotten. Serving with Thompson was an attractive opportunity for career officers. He clearly had money (he even lent it to his officers to tide them over until the regiment was complete), and he had friends in high places, suggesting that the regiment would have a future even after the American war ended. A better future for loyalists, for sure, than being abandoned in America or becoming refugees in England. Murray was able to make a good case to his brother officers, and with Thompson's backing was also able to buy up embryonic units that had been unable to reach full strength because the money of their backers had run out. Murray himself brought several recruits with him from a previous abortive venture. Officers who brought men with them were welcomed with open arms; others who had no following were so eager to become part of Thompson's attractive adventure that they paid—in at least one case contributing 500 guineas. As for the common soldiers, if nothing else, the bounty Thomson offered was enough to attract enlisted men, and in the confusion at the end of the war, in exchange for 10 guineas many soldiers seem to have been happy to desert their units and sign up with the King's American Dragoons, with the recruiting officer turning a blind eye to their transparent claims to be civilians. They would, of course, be equally happy to desert the dragoons if they could get away with it once they had their money, but at least for a while the numbers added up in Thompson's favor.

One way or another, Thompson's regiment was complete by the beginning of August 1782. At the end of the month, Sir Guy Carleton formally recorded in his general orders that Thompson and his officers were entitled to permanent rank in the British forces serving in America. The only snag was, the shooting war in America was over. The Whig party, under Lord Shelburne, was now in power and had formally ceased hostilities in North America while negotiating a settlement. But the French and their continental allies, eager to gain territory from Britain, were still a threat and a formal peace treaty would not be signed for more than another year. The army the regiment was now part of had nobody to fight. But fighting had never been the main reason for raising the regiment; it was there to ensure Thompson's future, both in the form of half-pay and by adding to his status. While it served in effect as an army of occupation in the months ahead, he lost no opportunity of burnishing his reputation and securing that future. What we know of him during those months comes mostly from his own writings, which we can be sure present him in the best possible light, but some of the shine is taken off by the occasional glimpses provided by other accounts.

The burnishing of the reputation of the regiment, and by implication of Thompson, had begun on August 1, when its colors were presented into the hands of Lieutenant Colonel Thompson by Prince William, the third son of the king. He would himself reign as William IV, and be succeeded by Queen Victoria, his niece. The young prince was just sixteen at the time and serving in the royal navy in a ship that happened to be visiting New York at the time. Thompson, seizing the opportunity, arranged and paid for the visit of William to review the regiment at its camp in a widely publicized grand pageant, where the assembled company feasted on a whole roast ox.

For the rest of 1782 and through the following winter, the King's American Dragoons were quartered in Huntington, Long Island, with very little to do. One thing Thompson did do was try to make contact with his family. In a letter to Sackville dated October 7, 1782, he says:[9]

I have not yet heard one syllable directly from New Hampshire tho' I have made many attempts. I begin to be at a loss to guess the reason for the dead silence. They must know I am here.

We are as baffled by this as Thompson was, because there is no evidence that his communications ever reached his wife. But the letter gives the lie to widespread claims, which can be traced back to Ellis, that he made no attempt to get in touch with his family at this time.

As was the custom with armies of the day, they lived off the land, taking whatever they needed with little regard for the civilian populace. Partly for sound military reasons, Thompson chose for the site of his fortified camp two acres of high ground around the First Presbyterian Church, a wooden structure that was torn down (by no means a unique incident among occupying armies of the day) to provide building materials. Apple trees and chestnut railings were cut down for firewood, and tombstones were used to make tables and ovens. Perhaps not too much credence should be placed on the story that loaves of bread baked by the soldiers and handed out to the locals were embossed with the reversed inscriptions from the gravestones, but the spread of the story gives some idea of the way people felt about the occupation.

Just across the water from Thompson's dragoons, close to Stamford, there was an American force under Major Benjamin Tallmadge, himself a Long Islander, who ran an efficient spy system on the island, and who in spite of the looming peace sent harassing expeditions in whaleboats to annoy the British. His agents reported that Thompson's troops "live upon the Inhabitants as they please, and commit great acts of Violence."[10] Thompson himself had two servants, six horses with a negro groom, and a carriage. He also had a new plan.

At the end of November 1782, the British agreed to peace terms with the Americans, but this deal was kept secret from the French, and the terms specified that it would only come into force when a treaty was signed with the French as well. Meanwhile, hostilities between Britain and France continued, with their focus in the West Indies. It would be logical for British forces pulled out from America to be sent there as reinforcements, and Thompson campaigned for the King's American Dragoons, augmented with other units, to be part of any such transfer. The augmented force, he argued, would justify having a full colonel (himself, of course) in command, with a lieutenant colonel (Murray) as second in command. Thompson was undoubtedly mainly concerned about his own future; but his efforts in 1783 did a great deal for the troops under his command, even if he was not successful in achieving all his objectives.

Thompson laid out his case to Carleton in a document dated March 14, 1783:[11]

> *That the Officers of the Kings American Dragoons are chiefly young Men of the first Families and Connections in North America, who at a very early Period of the War entered into the King's Service . . . they are all Americans; and have suffered very considerably by the Rebellion: That in the Event of Peace and the Independency of the American Provinces, all their Hopes of returning to their former Situations will be at an End; and they will be reduced to the greatest Distress; Their Friends involved in the Common Ruin will be unable to assist them; and having no Profession, but the Profession of Arms, in which they have been trained up from their Youth, they will be unable to provide for themselves by their Industry in any other Calling: That they are all passionately fond of the Service, and desirous of remaining in it, and are willing to go to any Quarter of the Globe, provided they can be employed.*

Thompson backed this up with detailed proposals and letters of recommendation that Carleton passed on to London with his approval. Carleton also formally listed the regiment as permanent, not merely a "hostilities only" force solely raised for the duration of the American war. But the authorities in London had far more to worry about than the fate of a small force of volunteers stranded in New York by the end of the war, and no replies were forthcoming. So Thompson arranged an official leave of absence, left his affairs in America in the hands of Edward Winslow, the muster master general of his regiment, and on April 11 set off to England to press his case. He would never return to the land of his birth.

In London, Thompson lobbied vigorously on behalf of himself and his regiment, gaining access to the powers that be through Viscount Sackville (the former Lord George Germain). By being on the spot and having this access, he was able to get the fate of the King's American Dragoons moved up the pecking order of petitions, but it quickly became clear that the war with France would soon be over and there would be no need for them in the West Indies. Disbandment of the regiment was inevitable, so it now became a question of obtaining the best terms he could for the disbandment. In particular, getting promoted to full colonel first, boosting his half-pay.

The first attempt at getting the promotion was rebuffed. On July 10, Lord North, now home secretary in a coalition government essentially headed by Charles Fox, received this negative response of the king to the suggestion: "I can see no real right to Mr. Thompson to obtaining the rank of Colonel, which ought to be granted with a most sparing hand; considering the few Years he has served that of Lieut. Colonel seems very sufficient."[12] But Thompson's influence and powers of persuasion were not exhausted, and although we do not know exactly what happened over the next few weeks, we get a clue from a letter he had sent to Carleton on July 6,[13] in which he says:

> *I took the liberty of soliciting the rank of Colonel of the King's American Dragoons, and that Major Murray might be promoted to the rank of lieutenant-colonel of the same; which request I flattered myself would not be thought unreasonable, as it was originally intended that*

there should be a colonel and a lieutenant-colonel to the regiment, and as your Excellency had given me reason to hope that you would have honoured me with the provincial rank of colonel had I embarked for the West Indies with the corps to the command of which you had appointed me.

It seems that it was the West Indies card that won the promotion. On August 8 the Secretary of State wrote to Carleton:[14]

Lieutenant-Colonel Thompson having been particularly distinguished by you in the appointment to the command of the corps of provincial troops intended to be sent upon service in the West Indies, (which corps, had it embarked, would, agreeably to the King's commands signified by the late Secretary of State in his letter of the 3rd of January last, have been placed upon the British establishment), and as it appears by your letter of the 15th of June that his conduct has met with your full approbation, and that you consider him to be an officer possessing an uncommon share of merit in his profession, the King, for these reasons, has consented to him being appointed, by commission of you, Colonel of the King's American Dragoons.

To celebrate his promotion, Thompson, dressed in his colonel's uniform, had his portrait painted by no less than Thomas Gainsborough.

The appointment came in the nick of time. On August 17 Carleton issued an order for all the men under his command who wished to be discharged in North America rather than going to England as refugees to prepare for a move to Nova Scotia,[15] and in October the King's American Dragoons were formally disbanded some way up the St. John River, north of the Bay of Fundy. The officers, thanks to Thompson, had their half-pay, although Murray, in spite of Thompson's efforts, did not get his promotion. They were also, at Thompson's suggestion, each allowed to take a horse with them. Noncommissioned officers received a grant of two hundred acres of land, while privates received one hundred acres. As Carleton wrote to Thompson on October 10, "Your zeal and assiduity on this occasion appear to have been such as your friends might have expected."[16] After just sixteen months of "active" service, Colonel Benjamin Thompson himself officially retired on half-pay on October 25, 1783, some seven weeks after the signing of the Treaty of Paris that formally ended the war in America. But by then he had already left England at the start of his next adventure.

PART III

Bavarian Rhapsody

CHAPTER 5

From Colonel to Count

THOMPSON'S INITIAL PLAN WAS TO BECOME A SOLDIER OF FORTUNE IN Europe, where trouble was always brewing. "Should there be a War," he wrote to Murray on September 10, 1783, "I shall engage in it, on one side or the other. I don't care a farthing which."[1] The same day he wrote to Edward Winslow with a more detailed itinerary:[2]

> *I shall leave London on Sunday next, shall cross from Dover to Calais, and from thence shall pass through Flanders to Strasbourg, and by Ulm and Munich to Vienna where I propose to Winter. In the Spring I shall Visit Hungary, Bohemia, Saxony and the King of Prussia's Dominions, & from Berlin I shall probably shape my course toward old England.*

Almost inevitably, however, these plans would be altered by events.

Because officers in European armies were expected in those days to supply their own horses, he had three of the finest and his own groom traveling with him, as well as his personal servant. The fact that he spoke no German and hardly any French doesn't seem to have affected his boundless optimism that something would turn up—and it did.

Not everyone, though, was impressed by Thompson. The only other gentlemen on board for the short crossing to France were Henry Laurens, a former president of the American Congress who was on his way to meet Benjamin Franklin in Paris, and Edward Gibbon, then working on the second half of his epic *Decline and Fall of the Roman Empire*. It

67

was Gibbon who started a letter to Lord Sheffield while still in harbor at Dover:[3]

> *What a cursed thing to live in an island! This step is more awkward than the whole journey. The triumvirate of this memorable embarkation will consist of the grand Gibbon, Henry Laurens, Esq., President of the Congress, and Mr. Secretary, Colonel, Admiral, Philosopher Thompson, attended by three horses, who are not the most agreeable fellow-passengers. If we survive, I will finish and seal my letter at Calais.*

Which gives you some idea of the way Thompson presented himself to the world. In fact, because of adverse weather the boat ended up at Boulogne. Thompson may not have impressed Gibbon, but he soon made a bigger impact when he visited Strasbourg. We have to be wary of accepting all of the story of what followed there at face value, because it comes from Thompson himself, as told to the Swiss polymath Marc-Auguste Pictet some years later. Pictet was an admirer of Thompson who corresponded with him extensively over the years, interviewed him,[4] and published a biography of Thompson in the *Bibliothèque Britannique*, from which this story is taken. But as Gibbon's description reminds us, Thompson was always ready to maximize his achievements, and Pictet was hardly a critical reporter. Nevertheless, in view of what happened later it is clear that something like the encounter reported by Pictet did happen.

According to this account, while Thompson was in Strasbourg, Prince Maximilian of Deux-Ponts, the younger brother of the local ruler, Charles II, who was also a field marshall in the French army, was reviewing his troops at a parade when he noticed a striking figure, mounted on a fine horse and wearing a scarlet uniform, watching the proceedings. The striking individual was, of course, Thompson, dressed in his best colonel's rig, making sure that everyone noticed him. Intrigued by the presence of a senior British officer so soon after the end of the latest war between Britain and France, the prince spoke to him and, when he learned that Thompson had been involved in the war in America, introduced him to officers from his own regiment who had been fighting on the other side and were present at Yorktown. Thompson seems to have managed to give them the impression that he had been actively involved in the war, and after several days of friendly discussion of the recent military activity in America, Thompson went on his way with a cordial letter of introduction from Maximilian to his uncle, Carl Theodor, the elector of Bavaria, who ruled from Munich. This was the key that would open the door to the rest of Thompson's life.

Deux-Ponts (or Zweibrücken in German) was a small duchy just to the north of Alsace-Lorraine, but its prince was an important man because his brother was the heir to his uncle in Munich,[5] and Bavaria was a major part of the agglomeration of more or less independent states known as the Holy Roman Empire. The "empire" was nominally ruled by an emperor who was elected by the heads of the main states, hence Carl Theodor's title. But boundaries and spheres of influence were far from clear cut in the vast area covered by these states, which, as historians like to quip, was neither holy, nor Roman, nor an empire.

The most important component of the empire (the lowercase seems appropriate) was Austria, which controlled not only the German-speaking region of the modern state, but Hungary, Northern Italy, and part of the Balkans. Next came Prussia, in the east of modern Germany but, like Austria, also ruling non-German regions, in this case modern Poland. Bavaria was about the third most important state in the empire going by population, although Saxony might have disputed that—they each had about two million people. But Bavaria's influence had been boosted when Carl Theodor came to the throne. He had originally been the ruler of a group of duchies called the Palatinate, which formed a straggling group of mini states running from Belgium to Austria roughly along the French and Swiss borders. When he inherited Bavaria in 1778, he retained the Palatinate. He also retained the French language and customs he was used to, choosing not to use the Germanic version of his name, Karl Theodor, and loathing Munich. He was an absolute ruler of a poor, backward state, full of ignorant and superstitious people who still believed in evil spirits. Until Thompson came along—and even afterward—the biggest influence on the elector was the Jesuit priest who was his confessor. It would be Thompson, more than anyone else, who would bring Bavaria out of its Dark Ages. But when he first met Carl Theodor, neither of them could have foreseen that.

That meeting took place when Thompson spent five days in Munich on his way, as originally planned, to Vienna, the capital of Austria. His scientific curiosity was revived when he met up there with Jan Ingen-Housz, another Fellow of the Royal Society, whom he had known in London. Ingen-Housz, like Thompson, had a special interest in gunpowder, and had carried out many explosive experiments, so there was plenty for them to discuss. But it was there that discussions of another kind saw Thompson's plans begin to change, as he perceived opportunities for himself in Munich, and as his thoughts of becoming a soldier of fortune faded in the light of advice he received from an unlikely source.

In Vienna, Thompson met a retired Austrian general, Heinrich Otto von Burghausen, and his wife at a party. Frau Burghausen seems to have taken him under her wing, and offered some words of wisdom that he took to heart. As he told Pictet:

> *I owe it to a beneficent Deity that I was cured in season of this martial folly. I met, at the house of the Prince de Kaunitz, a lady, aged seventy years, of infinite spirit and full of information. She was the wife of General Berghausen. The Emperor, Joseph II, came often to pass the evening with her. This excellent person conceived a regard for me; she gave me the wisest advice, made my ideas take a new direction, and opened my eyes to other kinds of glory than that of victory in battle.*

Munich offered the best prospects for those other kinds of glory. Apart from the friendly relations he had already begun to establish with Carl Theodor, there was another reason to return. Thompson carried with him to Vienna letters of introduction to the British ambassador, Sir Robert Keith, who soon appreciated (if he had not known already) that Thompson's background could make him a useful informer at the court in Munich, or, indeed, anywhere else he might end up. With a secret arrangement between the two in place, Thompson moved on to Italy, where he spent December 1783 and January 1784 taking in the sights like any gentleman on the Grand Tour, and also checking out the port of Trieste (then under Austrian control), where he uncovered sensitive military information that he duly reported back to Keith, confirming his worth as a spy. Then, it was back to Munich.

Frustratingly, we do not know exactly what passed between Thompson and the elector, but we do know the outcome. On February 6 he wrote to Keith,[6] "I have made a bold stroke and it has succeeded. I offered my Service here and it has been accepted, and accepted in the most flattering manner." Carl Theodor seems to have been eager for Thompson to join his retinue, but let it be known that his new protégé's position at the court in Munich would be greatly enhanced if George III could be persuaded to confer some honor on him. In any case, Thompson, as a half-pay officer in the British army, had to visit London to obtain permission to serve a foreign potentate. As it happened, the British were eager at the time to encourage friendly relations with Bavaria, which was traditionally in the French sphere of influence, and Britain was often at war with France. Having Bavaria as an ally, or at least not hostile, would be something of a coup—to that end Thomas Walpole had just been sent to represent British interests in Munich. There was also the unmentioned possibility of having a spy at the court of the elector. So the king not only gave permission for Thompson to enter the service of Carl Theodor, he was also "graciously pleased," as the official document puts it,[7] "to honour him with a Public and very distinguished mark of his Royal Approbation, and favour, by conferring on him the honour of Knighthood" with effect from February 23, 1784.

So after packing up in London and arranging for his things to be sent on, it was as Sir Benjamin that Thompson, now just turning thirty-one, returned to Munich. When Edward Winslow, by then busy helping to establish the Canadian Province of New Brunswick, heard the news, he wrote to a friend:[8]

> *Well done Sir Benjamin! The next news we hear will probably be that he has mounted a Baloon—taken his flight from Bavaria—and is Chief Engineer to an Aerial Queen.*

What actually happened was almost as remarkable.

At first, Thompson settled in relatively quietly as a newcomer to the Bavarian court. His role as aide-de-camp was fairly nebulous, and one of his main official occupations was as tutor to young Count von Bretzenheim, an illegitimate son of Carl Theodor. The elector himself ran the kind of old-fashioned court in which savants were prized as symbols of the ruler's (real or imagined) intellect and sophistication, much like a royal artist. Somebody who was simultaneously a colonel in the British army, a Knight of the Realm, a Fellow of the Royal Society, and a genuine natural philosopher was an exotic embellishment to the court in Munich, even if he had contributed nothing of a practical nature.

Thompson certainly fit in with Carl Theodor's idea of government. His French contemporary Georges Cuvier later wrote,[9]

> *He thought it was not wise or good to intrust to men in the mass, the care of their own well being. The right, which seems so natural to them, of judging whether they are wisely governed, appeared to him to be a fictitious fancy born of false notions of enlightenment. . . . He regarded the government of China as coming nearest to perfection, because in giving over the people to the absolute control of their intelligent men alone, and in lifting each of those who belonged to this hierarchy on the scale according to the degree of his education, it made, so to speak, so many millions of arms the passive organs of the will of a few sound heads.*

As one of those few sound heads, Thompson would soon be in a position to put this philosophy into practice. But first he had to settle in and gain the confidence of the elector. He was given the use of half of a great house (the other half being occupied by the Russian ambassador), with an appropriate retinue of servants; he learned German; and on June 5, 1784, he gave his oath of allegiance as a Bavarian officer, becoming a Bavarian colonel, but one without a regiment. While this was going on, the trickle of information he was supplying to Sir Robert Keith dried up. Although Thompson had written to Keith on May 28, 1784, confirming that "I shall not fail to acquaint you with every thing new and interesting that turns up here, or that comes to my knowledge from other parts,"[10] within a year Keith was so convinced that Thompson had gone native that the British government told Thomas Walpole, their man in Munich, to keep an eye on Thompson and report his activities back to them.

Thompson had certainly gone native in embracing some of the standards of the Bavarian court, which had a relaxed attitude to sexual liaisons between partners of equal social status. Enjoying the sexually liberated atmosphere of 1780s Bavaria he had affairs with (among others) two sisters, the Countesses Baumgarten and Nogarola; the first of these (who was also a mistress of Carl Theodor) became the mother of his daughter Sophia in 1788. The sisters, Josepha and Maddelana (often called Mary), were members of a wealthy family, the Lerchenfelds, who owned land in both Italy and Germany. Their grand house in Munich was one of the focuses of Bavarian high society, to which Thompson naturally gravitated. Josepha, the elder daughter, had married Count Hermann Joseph Baumgarten when she was seventeen and he was fifty-four (he died in a drowning accident in 1790). Very soon afterward she had a son, named Karl Theodor after the elector and Joseph after her husband; it was widely rumored that the elector was the father of the boy, and the marriage may have been arranged to legitimize the child. Whatever the reason, the marriage seems to have been, like many aristocratic marriages, one of convenience rather than passion, with the couple on friendly terms and openly having affairs. Josepha was a favorite mistress of the elector, and some of her other children were probably fathered by him. She simultaneously became a favorite of Thompson, soon after his arrival at court, and his daughter Sophia (Sophy) was born on August 17, 1788.[11]

The attraction between Thompson and Josepha seems to have been largely physical, but his relationship with her younger sister was different. Mary was only fourteen when he first met her, in 1784, and never became a renowned beauty like her elder sister, although she was slim and good looking. There is no suggestion that her physical relationship with Thompson began at such an early age, but she was intelligent and interested in his plans. They became friends first and lovers later, after she became Countess Nogarola on her marriage to Count Dinardano Nogarola. Thompson and the countess remained close friends for many years, and she helped him with translations of his works and the phrasing of his writing in French and German.

To an outside observer, Thompson's life in Munich from 1784 to 1788 must have seemed largely one of idle pleasure, like the lives of most of the members of the court. All the while, though, he was learning about Bavaria, and at the request of the elector working out ways to make the army, in particular, more efficient. It was when he put these schemes into practice that he ended up revolutionizing Bavarian society, and developing revolutionary ideas in science.

The scientific experimenting started first. In 1785, the elector summered in Mannheim, intending to spend some time visiting his Palatinate territories. This sent political alarm bells ringing because Carl Theodor had a longstanding dream of exchanging a chunk of Bavaria, which he had no love for, for provinces Austria ruled in the low countries. This would have extended the Palatinate, which he much preferred, to Brussels and Antwerp, giving him an opportunity to move back to the region he loved. The Austrians were happy to make the swap, which would have given them more territory on the border of Austria rather than a cut-off fragment of empire. But it had been vigorously opposed in the past, particularly by the British and the Prussians, and this final (as it turned out) attempt to revive the plan was also squashed. The political machinations came to nothing, but while he was in Mannheim with the elector and with time on his hands Thompson was elected as a member of the Academy of Sciences there, a thriving institution set up by the previous elector. There, he found a first-class instrument maker called Charles Artaria, and with his aid began a series of experiments on the way heat is propagated through various materials.

No particularly dramatic discoveries came out of these early experiments, although Thompson did find that dry air is a better insulator of heat than damp air is, and he obtained enough data to produce a pair of scientific papers, published by the Royal Society in 1786 and 1787. In the second of these, he wanders into speculation about the role of the ocean as "the great reservoir and equalizer of Heat; and its benign influence in preserving a proper temperature in the atmosphere"[12] by keeping coastal regions cool in summer and warm in winter. But we get an insight into his thinking, typical of many eighteenth-century natural philosophers, when he goes on to attribute this to "the wisdom and goodness of Providence [God]" in making the ocean so "wonderfully well-adapted" to bring "new life and vigour both to the animal and vegetable creation" on land. These are certainly appropriate comments for a natural philosopher working at the court of a staunchly Roman Catholic ruler, but in various places in his writings Thompson makes it clear that he genuinely believes in a Deity, and that discoveries made by science testify to the glory of God's Creation.

The summer of 1785 was also notable for further signs of Thompson's favor with Carl Theodor. On July 10, he was appointed as Chamberlain, a title that carried no specific duties but that signified that the holder was a member of the elector's inner circle. In the same month, the king of Poland, Stanislaus II, appointed Thompson to the Royal Order of Saint Stanislaus, making him a Knight of the White Eagle. It may seem bizarre that Stanislaus II should have taken this action, but it appears to have been a favor to Carl Theodor, who was not allowed to bestow this kind of honor on a non-Catholic. The order was supposed to be for no more than a hundred knights, for distinguished service to Poland. But Stanislaus II didn't seem too bothered by either qualification, and handed it out widely. This rather diminished the prestige of the honor, but that did not bother Thompson, who wrote to Sackville:[13]

> *I can say with truth that I hardly know what there is left for me to wish for. Rank, Titles, Decorations, Litterary distinctions, with some degree of litterary, and some small degree of military fame I have acquired, (through your availing Protection), and the road is open to me for the rest. No man supports a better moral Character than I do, and no man is better satisfied with himself. . . . Look back for a moment my dearest friend upon the work of your hands—Je suis de votre ouvrage. Does it not afford you a very sensible pleasure to find that your Child has answered your Expectations?*

Alas, Sackville never read the letter. By the time it reached England he was dead. But his protégé no longer had any need of his patronage.

With his position secure, Thompson now found time to do something to help his mother, back in America. But he took elaborate precautions to make sure that his wife, Sarah, and daughter, Sally, knew nothing of his success, fearing that Lady Sarah (as she now was, but did not know) would come after him to demand her share. He must have been aware that she had managed to run through most of her fortune and was independently minded enough to turn up at the court in Munich, where her presence would certainly cramp his style. But his response gives us a glimpse of his dark side. Instead of sending money direct to his mother, now Ruth Pierce and a widow for a second time, Thompson contacted Reverend Samuel Williams, the mentor who had persuaded him that his vocation lay in teaching and had thereby inadvertently set him on the path to fame and fortune. Williams was supposed to pass on £100 sent by Thompson to Mrs. Pierce, without anyone else getting wind of it. He duly reported success, and described the gratitude of Thompson's mother. Unfortunately, this was not the whole story. With a wife and five children to support, Williams had turned to embezzlement and fraud to augment his income. When this was discovered he had to escape in 1788 to Vermont, which was not then one of the United States, to avoid prosecution. All Mrs. Pierce had actually received was 30 American dollars. Thompson's love of secrecy had backfired.

But his work as the court's tame philosopher was thriving, and he was developing his skill as a popularizer of science. One thread of his investigations involved the strength and other properties of silk, developing from his experiences supplying material to the British army. Silk was starting to make a modest contribution to the economy of Bavaria, where the presence of a pool of desperately poor people provided the cheap labor force needed to feed the silkworms with mulberry leaves round the clock. Thompson's work did not lead to any great scientific breakthroughs, but a paper published in the *Philosophical Transactions* in 1787[14] demonstrates how he must have put his message across to Carl Theodor and his court. He tells us that "if a Silk Gown worn by a lady weighs 28 ounces it is very certain that she carries upon her back upwards of 2000 miles in length of silk, as spun by the worm"; that "a man might actually carry in his Pockets a thread long enough to reach round the world"; and most dramatically that

a quantity of silk sufficient to load an English broad-wheeled-wagon drawn by eight Horses would contain a length of thread so great that a Canon Bullet flying continually day and night with the rapidity with which it leaves the mouth of the Piece would take rather more than fourteen years to pass from one end of it to the other.

An experiment from which Thompson drew entirely the wrong conclusion enhanced his reputation in Munich even further. He had noticed that bubbles of gas formed on fibers of silk soaking in water on a sunny windowsill. This was just at the time other natural philosophers were investigating the bubbles given off in similar circumstances by green plants, and discovering that they were "dephlogisticated air," or oxygen—produced, we now know, by photosynthesis. Thompson thought that the same process was at work in the fibers of silk, and carried out careful experiments that confirmed that he was obtaining dephlogisticated air—in one simple test, a smoldering splinter of wood plunged into the gas bursts into flame as it encounters the oxygen. But silk fibers cannot produce oxygen by photosynthesis, and the modern explanation of his results is that the bubbles were formed by algae growing on the fibers. Whatever the origin of the gas, though, when Thompson set up his apparatus in the garden of the elector's palace he could show an admiring crowd of courtiers how he produced the bubbles as if by magic on the fibers of silk, collected the gas in a glass vessel, and used it to reignite a candle that had just been snuffed out. The philosopher was clearly worthy of a place at court.

In 1788, however, Thompson was ready to go beyond impressive scientific party tricks and get down to his real work in Bavaria, reorganizing the army and through that reforming the state. As Ellis has commented, "There was no State in Christendom at the time which offered a fairer field for the economical and reformatory enterprise of a man with the genius and proclivities of Sir Benjamin Thompson." Things were so bad that they could only get better. The army certainly needed reorganizing, and Carl Theodor had this in mind when he brought Thompson into his inner circle. He probably also had in mind that if the reforms did not work out, all the blame would rest upon the shoulders of a foreigner, who could be sent back to England in disgrace, leaving the elector untarnished. But Thompson had no intention of failing. For four years, Sir Benjamin had been learning the language, enjoying the customs of the court, and carrying out some modest scientific experimenting. But all along he had also been studying the military machine (such as it was) of his employer, and working out how to improve it. Now it was time to act.

The Bavarian army at the beginning of 1788 was poorly paid and equipped, badly fed and clothed, and had low morale. A quarter of its eighteen thousand strength were officers, including several general field marshals and an admiral in charge of the "navy"—a couple of boats on the Rhine. They enjoyed their status without any real responsibility. Many of the ordinary soldiers were convicted criminals, who were sentenced to army service as an alternative to prison, and most of the rest shared these criminal tendencies, even if they hadn't been convicted. With nothing to do most of the time, they acted more like bandits than protectors of the citizenry, stealing, begging, and terrorizing the populace. As a fighting force, they were pretty much useless, leaving Carl Theodor in a weak position in the power politics of late eighteenth-century Europe. In February 1788, after nearly four years of study, Thompson submitted his plan for reforming the army to the elector. It's a sign of how desperate the situation had become that these wide-ranging proposals were immediately accepted. Thompson was appointed as minister of war, minister of police, and state councillor; promoted to major general; and given carte blanche to sort out the mess. And one other thing. The military budget was not to be increased, but if Thompson made any savings he could keep them for himself. It never occurred to the elector that he would turn the army into a profitable organization. In April 1788, when Thompson had just turned thirty-five, Walpole reported to London that "the Elector has given General Thompson the entire and absolute Direction of the Execution of his Plan,"[15] which encompassed the Palatinate as well as Bavaria.

Thompson's avowed aim was "to unite the interest of the soldier with the interest of civil society, and to render the military force, even in time of peace, subservient to the public good."[16] His attitude was more like that of a benevolent slave owner eager to ensure the health of his slaves in order to maximize their productivity than that of a socialist with an idealistic commitment to improving the lot of the poor, but his reforms were comprehensive and effective. Before, the soldiers were paid just about enough to cover the cost of their food, which they had to supply for themselves, but they also had to buy their own uniforms and equipment, which they could only pay for by working as laborers on contracts arranged by their officers, who took a cut. Under Thompson's system, their pay was increased, they would be supplied with uniforms, and they would be paid directly for outside work. The officers' pay would be increased to allow for their own loss of income. Instead of being moved about the country almost at whim, soldiers were stationed in permanent bases so that their families could live near them. Not just the soldiers but their wives and children as well were encouraged to take the opportunity to learn to read and write, using free books, pens, and paper. In a telling example of Thompson's love of efficiency and attention to detail, he directed that the used paper should then be collected and used for making cartridges. Instead of idling their free time away, soldiers were offered paid work outside their military duties on road building and other civil projects. Sporting activities were encouraged and military bands established. And all of this would be achieved without any cost to the government, thanks to the two greatest reforms, involving food and clothing.

It's obvious why all this would appeal to the common soldiers. But how did Thompson get the officer corps to support these changes? He simply announced that all profiteering by the officers would end, and that any infringements of the rule would be cracked down on hard. As he expected, large numbers of corrupt officers resigned, thinking that he would be left in the lurch and have to go back on his word. Instead he promoted officers who had remained to fill the gaps where necessary. He had at once thinned out the top-heavy officer corps, gotten rid of troublemakers, and provided himself with a loyal band of followers who owed their positions to him. This included six major generals promoted to lieutenant general, twenty-two colonels promoted to major general, thirty-three lieutenant colonels promoted to colonel, and more than a hundred second lieutenants promoted to first lieutenant. Now the plan could be put into action with the support of his officers.

Instead of buying all of their food, at the cheapest prices, each of the now permanent garrisons cultivated its own vegetable garden, often developing previously unproductive wasteland for their use. Thompson (who so nearly became a gentleman farmer himself) provided instructions on which vegetables to grow, crop rotation, and other good practices. He also introduced the potato, a crop regarded with suspicion by many Europeans at the time, and after a series of experiments invented a cheap but nutritious and palatable potato-based soup to feed large numbers of men at modest cost.

But it was his study of the materials used for military clothing that best shows Thompson's application of science to his plan for the army. He was interested in how efficiently different kinds of material trap heat, and carried out experiments not just on different materials but with the same material arranged in different ways—close packed layers of cloth, loosely layered, wet or dry, and so on. He found that materials such as feathers or fur in which layers of air are trapped make better insulators, because of the insulating properties of the air itself. This was a major discovery, published by Thompson in the *Philosophical Transactions* in 1792, and led to him being awarded in the same year the Copley Medal, one of the most prestigious prizes of the Royal Society, for "his various Papers on the Properties and Communication of Heat." It also meant that he could design uniforms made of cool cotton for summer wear and warm woolen ones for winter wear.

Who, though, was to make the new uniforms? The traditional civilian contractors were reluctant to change their practices, and their charges were exorbitant. Thompson's next scheme solved both problems, and also cleaned up the streets of the cities. This was where his role of minister of police came in handy. He decided to round up the army of beggars, estimated at 5 percent of the population, and put them to work making uniforms in workhouses. But not the kind of workhouses we read about in Dickens. Thompson provided his workers with (by the standards of the day) clean, comfortable accommodations; decent working conditions; opportunities for education; and decent food. And they were paid.

Children were required to take lessons, attending school regularly for an hour in the morning and an hour in the afternoon every day; arguably, this was the first state education system in the world. Thompson later summed up his far-sighted approach:

> *To make vicious and abandoned people happy, it has been generally supposed necessary first to make them virtuous. But why not reverse this order? Why not make them first happy, and then virtuous?*

It worked. In a military-style operation on New Year's Day 1790, the army assisted the police in arresting every beggar, and the following day they were put to work. Thompson himself, not afraid to demonstrate his role, personally made the first arrest. Equally willing to put his money where his mouth was, Thompson partly funded the social experiment himself, but within a few years it was showing a profit. The regime was hard, but fair. Fit people (men, women, and children over the age of five, allocated tasks according to their ability) were required to work at their benches for twelve hours or more a day, but the elderly, sick, and infirm were also provided with food as long as they could contribute something from home. And the food really was decent fare, if dull. Thompson describes it as "a wholesome and nourishing repast consisting of about a pound and a quarter, avoirdupois weight, of a very rich soup of peas and barley mixed with cuttings of white bread, and a piece of excellent rye bread weighing seven ounces, which last they commonly put in their pockets and carried home for their supper." Children received the same ration, and a mother with several young children was allowed a full ration for each of them. It certainly beat starving on the streets.[17]

As well as making military uniforms, before long the workhouses were turning out winter coats for sale to the public. The scheme was such a success that before long a system of piecework was developed, allowing anyone to get raw materials from the workhouse, make up the items at home, and be paid in return. After six years, Thompson reported that the Munich workhouse had produced a profit of 100,000 florins. But money wasn't everything. He also wrote, "The pleasure I have had in the success of this experiment is much easier to be conceived than described; would to God that my success might encourage others to follow my example."

As former beggars were turned into happy, productive citizens and returned to the community, Thompson's popularity among the people soared, although this roused jealousy in court circles that stored up trouble for him later. His popularity was further increased by his decision to create what is still known as the English Garden in Munich. He persuaded the elector to give up a private hunting ground, the army provided the labor (for which the soldiers received extra pay), and in 1791 what was regarded as the finest public park in Europe—two kilometers long and one wide, larger than New York's Central Park—was opened to all.

Thompson's restless drive for efficiency in feeding his troops and workers also provided benefits for the population at large. Before his innovations, in Bavaria and everywhere else food was still cooked over open fires, with most of the heat wasted—the quip was that the fire cooked the cook more than it cooked the food. It was Thompson who invented the kitchen range, the forerunner of the AGA, where the fire is enclosed in its own compartment (or compartments) and the heat is transmitted through the fabric of the stove to the ovens or to hot plates. He also, over time, designed many items of kitchen equipment, including the pressure cooker and a drip coffeepot, as well as whole kitchens, and a portable stove for use by the army when in the field. This interest in kitchen efficiency also led him into a long investigation of the amount of heat produced by different kinds of fuel, which eventually resulted in the design of a small device, known as a calorimeter, that measured accurately how much heat was released by burning a certain amount of each substance, such as wood, charcoal, or coal. Thompson was also interested in improving the light inside buildings, for the very practical reason that this would enable his workforce to work longer hours, and developed several kinds of improved oil lamp. Along the way he realized that he needed some standard against which to measure the brightness of different lamps, and chose a particular kind of candle. In 1790 he wrote:

To fill the important office of a standard light with which all others are compared, I have chosen a wax candle of the first quality, just

*eight-tenths of an English inch in diameter, and which when burning
with a clear and steady flame has been found to consume very uni-
formly one hundred and eight grains Troy of wax per hour.*

This "standard candle" became the accepted international standard
for measuring brightness until well into the twentieth century, and is the
reason why some flashlights today are still described as having a million
candlepower—this literally means they are as bright as a million of the
candles used by Thompson in 1790. It is a perfect example of the way
Thompson based all his work on precise and accurate measurements,
part of the revolution in the way science is done that was occurring at
that time.

But he was always interested in the practical application of science,
not just the idea of abstract scientific enquiry. One of his lesser known
contributions was to introduce the first Boulton & Watt steam engine
into Germany, to pump water from wells into a reservoir in Mannheim.
At Thompson's instigation, the engine was ordered from Birmingham in
April 1791, and arrived in July. Arguably, this was the first step in the
industrialization of the Rhine region. He also set up a state-sponsored
fire insurance system, paid for out of taxes, so there would be fewer
homeless beggars on the streets. All very forward looking; but in one
respect Thompson was still a man of his time.

Like most of his aristocratic contemporaries, Thompson believed that
the "higher orders" of society were naturally superior to the common folk
by virtue of their birth, while the poor were poor because they had been
born with less intelligence and other abilities and could not improve their
lot (it doesn't seem to have occurred to him that he was living proof that
this was not always the case). Whether this was true or not, the civil and
military leaders of society came from the supposedly higher orders of
that society. But in the free and easy sexual environment of Munich at
that time, there was a high illegitimacy rate even among the aristocracy,
and "natural-born" children were often placed in poorhouses or given to
servants to raise as their own. Thompson saw this as a loss of potential
leaders of society. His response was to set up a house for ladies where
they could give birth, and a school for the boys they produced—girls, of

course, were not considered worth educating. He called this "a nursery for genious." The long-term aim, which never came to fruition because of the political turmoil of the ensuing years, was to keep track of the boys and "mark those who discover talents peculiarly useful to any particular department of public employment."

Even with all this going on, Thompson continued to work for the elector on the diplomatic front (or rather, in the diplomatic shadows). By the early 1790s, France was in the turmoil of revolution, and the Duke of Deux-Ponts/von Zweibrücken tried to use the opportunity to enhance his status. The duke would become the elector of Bavaria on Carl Theodor's death, but his own duchy had been under French control for a long time, and he wanted the elector to act with other German powers to bring it back into the Holy Roman Empire. Thompson was the elector's secret envoy in this scheming, which was overtaken by the ongoing developments in France and came to nothing. He was also involved in other secret missions, but by their very nature the details have not been recorded—what we know about the Deux-Ponts affair comes mostly from reports in the Public Record Office from British spies in Munich.

Hardly surprisingly, further honors were heaped upon Thompson at this time. On a visit to Berlin in 1787, he had been elected as a member of the Prussian Academy of Sciences, and in May 1789 he became a foreign member of the American Academy of Arts and Sciences. In March 1790 he had been appointed as privy councillor, and later the same year Carl Theodor awarded him a pension for life. In February 1792, he became a lieutenant general of artillery, chief of state, and head of the general staff. He was the second most powerful man in Bavaria. The following month came the cherry on top of the icing on the cake. On March 1, 1792, the Holy Roman Emperor, Leopold II, died. The next emperor would have to be chosen by the electors, in much the same way that a new pope is chosen by the college of cardinals, so there was an inevitable interregnum before the coronation of his successor, Francis II, on July 14. Carl Theodor, as one of the senior electors, briefly had much of the imperial responsibility (such as it was), including the power to bestow honors. In May 1792 he took the opportunity to elevate Thompson to the rank of count of the Holy Roman Empire. Showing that he had not forgotten his roots—and in particular the place where his rise to fame and fortune began—for his new name Thompson chose Rumford, the original name of the town where he first became a gentleman. From now on he would be known as Count Rumford—or in German, Reichsgraf von Rumford.[18] But the circumstances in Bavaria would soon be changing, and the new count was becoming exhausted by the effort he had been putting in since early 1788. For some time, he had been prone to bouts of ill health, suffering from what he called "putrid bilious disorders," which may be an indication of stomach ulcers, and his workload in the late 1780s and early 1790s had exacerbated the problem. Within a year, at the age of forty he would be on his travels once again, although, as it turned out, he had not quite finished with Bavaria, nor Bavaria with him.

There and Back Again or a Peripatetic Scientist

IT WAS A COMBINATION OF ILL HEALTH AND A CHANGE IN THE POLITI-
cal winds that set Rumford, as we shall now call him, on his travels again.
The ill health was genuine, but the politics may have been more important. Although Rumford had done wonders turning the army into citizens
and using them to clean up Bavaria, and although his English Garden
ensured his popularity with the people, there was growing opposition
among the establishment to the power and influence being wielded by
this outsider who had become the favorite of the elector. There was also
the small matter that in October 1792 the army of revolutionary France
invaded the Rhineland, and after defeating the Austrians took over
Belgium. There was now a direct threat to Bavaria at a time when the
army had become more of a police force than a fighting force. Rumford
was not seen as the right man to run the army in time of war. Equally,
Rumford may have felt that if Austria was going to take over Bavaria, he
would rather be somewhere else.

About the same time, he had a letter from his daughter Sarah, now
known as Sally. It was the first news he had had from his family in many
years, and it told him that his wife had just died at the age of fifty-two,
following which Loammi Baldwin had given Sally her father's address.
Rumford hardly had time to digest the news before a young man called
George Stacey arrived in Munich asking for permission to marry Sally.
Although Stacey was a respectable lawyer and carried with him a letter

from Baldwin singing his praises, Rumford gave him short shrift and packed him off back to America. But at a time when he had to be moving on anyway, this combination of events seems to have started him thinking about returning to his roots himself, and on January 18, 1793, he wrote in a letter to Baldwin,

> *You could hardly conceive the heartfelt satisfaction it would give me to pay a visit to my native country. Should I be kindly received? Are the remains of party spirit and political persecution done away?*

The tour he soon embarked on may have been partially viewed by him as his opportunity to see the sights before bidding farewell to Europe.

On March 10, 1793, Thomas Walpole, still Britain's man in Munich, reported to his superiors:[1]

> *The Departure of General Count Rumford is what now chiefly occupies the Public here—Sometimes from real and sometimes from feigned sickness, he has not appeared at Court these last four months; yet he has frequently done business with the Elector during the course of that time, nor have I perceived any diminution of favour; but now I believe his influence is at end. He will not leave the Military upon a better [war] footing than he found it, as I think; but [his] Establishments of the Poor house and Military Academy [are] of real benefits to the Country.*

Six days later, "General Count Rumford" left Munich, heading for Italy in the style that befitted his new noble status. These were interesting times politically, and France was now at war with Britain and Holland, but the repercussions had not yet been felt where he was heading, and there was nothing to cramp his style. One carriage-load of servants traveled ahead of him to make preparations at his next planned stopping place, a couple of baggage carts followed in his wake carrying what he regarded as the bare necessities for a tour intended to last for about a year and a half, while in between Thompson relaxed in his own luxurious coach with whatever company he chose to take with him. This was pretty much the usual entourage for an aristocrat on the Grand Tour; but unlike most of those tourists Rumford was more interested in the latest scientific developments in Italy than in the ancient history of the country, and he carried out his own scientific experiments along the way.

Although we don't have a complete record of Rumford's travels at this time, we can pick up the scientific thread of the story in June 1793, when he met up with Charles Blagden in Milan. Blagden, who was Secretary of the Royal Society and knew Rumford from his time in London, was coming to the end of his own Grand Tour of Italy, and at the time was with Henry Temple, the second Viscount Palmerston, and his family. Rumford was duly introduced to them, and soon became firm friends with Lady Mary Palmerston, the viscount's second wife (his first wife had died in childbirth), who described him as "a great acquisition to our society."[2] Palmerston himself was an active Whig politician, who had voted in favor of ending the war with the American rebels; his son, the third viscount, would become the first liberal prime minister in 1859. It was with Blagden, however, that Rumford traveled some twenty miles south of Milan to the university town of Pavia to see the laboratory of Alessandro Volta, famous as the pioneering investigator of electricity and inventor of the electric battery, who had been elected as a Fellow of the Royal Society in 1792. The British visitors were treated to a demonstration of Luigi Galvani's discovery that the legs from a dead frog could be made to twitch by touching them with rods made from two different metals at the same time, but also to other experiments with electricity that did not involve living (or once-living) things; Blagden reported back to Joseph Banks[3] that

> *[Volta's] experiments proved that there is no particular animal electricity, and that the animals serve only the purpose of very delicate electrometers.*

This was one of the last stops for Blagden before he went back to England via Munich; in a letter to Blagden written on July 26, Rumford reminded him, "I beseech you, when you are in Munic that it is for the recovery of my health that I have the Electors permission to travel—You must therefore take care to make me sick enough, particularly if the Elector should ask after me."[4] This is as good an indication as any that at least at that time the sickness was more feigned than real, as Walpole had hinted.

Rumford's next stop was Verona, where the Countess Nogarola was staying with her children out of harm's way while her husband was busy in Mannheim making preparations for what seemed like the inevitable war. They traveled together widely in the north of Italy, but when he went south heading for Rome and Naples later in the year she stayed behind. He did not, however, lack congenial company. In October, having got as far as Florence, he again met up with the Palmerstons, probably not by coincidence. It has sometimes been assumed that Lady Mary became one of Rumford's many lovers, but there seems to be no evidence for this except that she was intelligent, extroverted, and fifteen years younger than her husband (twenty-eight to his forty-three at that time). What is definite is that she became one of Rumford's firmest friends and confidantes, and one of his most influential advisers. The depth of the relationship would be highlighted in a letter he sent to her in November 1793 when he was away in Pisa for a short visit. "I have been so long used to your agreeable company," he wrote, "that I really feel quite awkward when I am deprived of it, and going from you is so like going from home that it makes me feel quite lonesome and melancholy."[5] But he also wrote in the same letter about meeting Lady Bolingbroke, another British aristocrat on the Grand Tour, and visiting her often at her lodgings: "Luckily I leave Pisa soon, or I do not know what I might have been tempted to do to cheat away her tedious lingering hours."

Boredom was not, however, a problem for Rumford. Apart from his full social life, during the two months he spent in Florence, armed with an introduction from Volta he had access to the workshop of Gregorio Fontana, a renowned chemist and instrument maker, where he carried out several experiments, most notably concerning the colors of shadows. Jumping off from observations he had made in Munich that the shadow cast by the yellow flame of a candle looks blue, he established that this and other colored shadows are optical illusions (complementary colors) caused by the contrast the eye and brain perceives with the color of the flame that makes the shadow. When Rumford looked through a tube with a black interior so that he could only see the shadow, he saw no color even though his assistant insisted that it was bright blue.

The artistic center of Florence was an ideal place to extend this observation to the appearance of colored paints on canvas and paper, and Rumford soon showed that similar illusions could be obtained in that way. In a neat demonstration, he laid a large piece of black paper on the floor, placed a circular piece of pink paper on top of it, then took two slips of paper, one colored red and one gray, and put them next to each other in the middle of the circular piece of paper. When he looked between his fingers to exclude from view everything except the paper, he "had the pleasure to perceive that the slip of paper which was covered with a grey powder now appeared to be of a beautiful greenish blue colour."

The Palmerstons were then invited to come into the room and tell him which colored slip was brightest:

> *After looking at them for some time, and going round to view them from different sides, one of them answered "I don't know which of them is the brightest. The red is very bright, and so is the blue. But why do you ask that question?" When I told them there was no blue there, and that what they took to be blue was merely a deception, they did not believe me; but they were much surprised, and convinced that what I told them was true, when they saw on my removing the red slip that its companion which was left behind, instantly <u>faded</u> and lost its colour.*[6]

Blagden took Rumford's paper reporting this work back to London with him, commenting to Banks that "he shows neatly enough that the colours ascribed to these shadows depend entirely on comparing them with light of another colour."[7]

From Florence, Rumford moved on to Naples early in 1794, traveling through Pisa, Livorno, and Rome. His long letters to Lady Palmerston, who was already in the south, give us details of the journey and his social life, and he speculated on the best way to use the horses—by traveling all day at a slow pace, or by traveling quickly for a shorter time to allow them more rest. He was intrigued by the hot baths and springs at Baiae, but did no significant scientific work during his time in Naples. All too soon, as far as he was concerned, it was time to head back to Munich at the end of his "sick leave." But he was unsure of how he would be received there. On May 27, 1794, he wrote to Lady Palmerston:[8]

People will hardly believe I have been ill, I look so much better (they say) than I did when I was here last year. How the air of Bavaria will agree with me I don't know. But I own I am much afraid of the experiment, which however I must soon try.

Rumford had managed to extend his absence on a long visit to Countess Nogarola in Verona, justifying the months he spent there by applying the techniques he had used in establishing the poorhouse in Munich to two hospitals, La Pietà and La Misericordia. His main work was involved in building new kitchens, although as he wrote later,[9]

I had an opportunity of making myself acquainted with all the details of the clothing of the poor belonging to [La Pietà]; and I found that very great savings might be made in that article of expense. I made a proposal to the directors of that hospital to furnish them with clothing for their poor, ready made up, from the House of Industry at Munich.

And he summed up, "I hope soon to see the poor of Bavaria growing rich by manufacturing clothing for the poor of Italy." Which, of course, helped to justify the time spent in Verona.

It was Rumford's work on kitchens, though, that highlights his application of scientific thinking to everyday problems, and that helped to make him a household name. This work had begun in Munich before his holiday in Italy, and it continued after his return there, but it makes sense to describe it all in one place. He identified the main problem with the traditional cooking method that the fuel was burned in a long open grate, with pots and pans suspended above the flames or placed on stands in front of the fire. This involved a great waste of heat, which not only consumed more fuel than necessary for the cooking but made the conditions in the kitchen almost intolerable for the cooks. This was obvious to any-body; but it was Rumford who found the solution to the problem.

After carrying out experiments that proved that the heat of the fire was most efficiently passed on to a cooking pot by direct contact with the flame, not by the hot air from the fire, he devised a stove in which the fire was kept in an insulated box at the bottom of the stove, with a cooking pot nestling in the upper part of the stove, ensuring the flow of heat from the fire into the pot. He also established that more heat is lost up the chimney from one big fire than from a series of smaller fires through smaller flues, so his design could be adapted to provide a series of stoves—a range—with many small fires linked side by side, with several flues extending to the chimney. This was an immediate success, and on June 9, 1794, Rumford wrote to Lady Palmerston that "several Convents and private families are preparing to introduce my improvements in the economy of fuel." Then, he reluctantly made his way back to Munich.

The situation there was much as he had feared. Although his return from Italy had been greeted rapturously by huge crowds at a reception held in the English Garden, the elector was now in his seventies, and the various factions maneuvering for power and influence in the inevitable succession saw no place for Rumford in their plans. As far as real power was concerned he was now on the outside looking in, and although he was still well in with the elector, his working life over the next few months was concentrated chiefly on improving his kitchen designs and developing more efficient ways of feeding the poor, largely based on the nutritious soup he devised. There was, though, time for an active social life. Lady Palmerston was in Munich in the summer of 1794, and after she left they kept up a flow of correspondence, from which we learn among other things that the Countess Nogarola spent several weeks with Rumford in the autumn that year. There are references to time Rumford spent with his daughter Sophy—who was also, of course, Countess Nogarola's niece. And the letters also refer to the main topic of gossip at court. In the summer of 1794, Carl Theodor's wife had died, and at the age of seventy-one he promptly married a seventeen-year-old Austrian princess, in the hope of fathering a male heir. The inversion of their ages provoked many bawdy comments, and it was widely speculated at court that he would be happy if one of his friends were to help him by ensuring that his bride became pregnant. Lady Palmerston asked Rumford if he had been doing his duty in this regard, and he replied in the negative, but asserted that it was "more than likely" that somebody else had been doing so. Whether or not the rumors were true, the male heir failed to appear. Rumford also joked with Lady Palmerston about his own complicated love life, telling her that his daughter Sophy

> is as charming as ever, and often comes and dines with me. But the Prophecy of her Mothers Mother that her father and her Aunts Lover would renew an old connection with her younger Daughters elder Sister, is not likely to be verified.[10]

But Rumford was getting tired of his situation in Munich. Now in his forties, and perhaps partly stimulated by the contacts he had made in Italy, he began thinking of establishing his name for posterity. As his focus of attention increasingly turned to publishing his ideas about science, Rumford spent several months putting his papers in order and writing essays about his achievements. The Royal Society was the best place to promote his scientific achievements, especially in view of the turmoil in France at the time, and London the best place to get the essays published in English. The news that the great French scientist Antoine Lavoisier had gone to the guillotine in May 1794 can only have reinforced Rumford's view, shared with every other aristocrat in Europe, that Paris was a place to be avoided, at least for the time being. So he sought an opportunity to travel to London for an extended visit. In October 1795 Carl Theodor gave Rumford a leave of absence to travel to London for a six-month stay. Few people in Munich seriously expected him to return, and Rumford's correspondence, notably his letter to Loammi Baldwin in January 1793, suggests that he too regarded the six-month leave of absence as the precursor to a more permanent move, possibly even beyond the shores of England.

When Rumford arrived in London, he was the victim of a bizarre robbery. His coach was held up by a gang of robbers in the darkness of St. Paul's churchyard, and they made off with just one trunk from his luggage. The trunk contained many of Rumford's private papers, some, but fortunately not all, of his scientific notes, but none of the manuscripts of his essays. There has been speculation that the theft was planned by the British secret service, still suspicious of Rumford and eager to find out who he was working for now. On the other hand, it may just have been that the gang could only carry one trunk, and threw the papers away in disgust when they found nothing of value to them inside. If the British secret service was suspicious about Rumford, they were not alone. Far from being welcomed with open arms, he found that London society initially regarded him as something of a turncoat, who had been working for a foreign power not always entirely friendly to Britain. On November 6, 1795, he wrote to Lady Palmerston:

> *Never surely was a human being exposed to so much unmerited persecution. I now find the loss of my Papers was but a prelude to much more serious misfortunes which were to befall me upon my return to this Country. To this Country! Why did I ever see it? How much happier should I have been had I never quitted the peaceful habitation where I was born? There, at least my innocence would have been sufficient to protect me against the poisonous breath of slander. But here alass! There is no protection for me. No peace, but in the grave. Would to God my sufferings were at an end,—but the idea of leaving my reputation a prey to those infernal wretches who never cease to persecute me drives me to distraction.*

But this was a short-lived dark period in what turned out to be a triumphant return to the United Kingdom. Rumford threw himself into his work, promoting his kitchen reforms, preparing papers for publication, and finding an outlet for them in the firm of Cadell and Davies, of the Strand. By February 1796 he was writing to Lady Palmerston in a much happier mood:

> *You can hardly form any idea of the enthusiasm with which my schemes for making the Poor comfortable and happy have been received by many of the most worthy and benevolent Characters in*

*this Town. Mr. Wilberforce has come to a resolution to move heaven
and Earth, and what is still more, the House of Commons, to get my
System adopted throughout the Kingdom.*

Rumford was becoming widely recognized not only as a great scientist, often at the Royal Society and on intimate terms with Joseph Banks, but also as a social reformer; now he was even picking up the threads of his family life. In the mid-1790s, the turmoil in Europe and the on-again, off-again war with France had surprisingly little impact on the strata of society in which Rumford moved, and he was able to bring Sally, now in her twenty-second year, over from America. She arrived in London in March 1796, and proved something of a social embarrassment with her unpolished country ways, which Rumford sought to improve by sending her to a finishing school run by a French émigrée, the Marquise de Chabann. Her lack of sophistication was partly because her mother had been an invalid for much of her life, and Sally had largely been brought up, with plenty of love but few social graces, by a favored female slave in the household of an aunt. Rumford himself enjoyed socializing and renewing acquaintance with old friends such as Lady Palmerston, but gave priority to getting his essays published. The first of these described aspects of his work in Munich, but these were soon followed by an essay titled "Of Chimney Fire-places, with Proposals for Improving Them to Save Fuel; to Render Dwelling Houses More Comfortable and Salubrious, and Effectively to Prevent Chimneys from Smoking." This was an extremely practical application of Rumford's discovery of convection, and of the knowledge he had gained about the nature of heat.

Until that time, chimneys consisted of a simple vertical shaft above the fire. Cold air coming down the chimney would spread smoke out into the room, and without a steady draft of air through the fire and up the chimney the fuel would not burn efficiently. This not only failed to heat the room effectively, but contributed to a pall of smoke that lay over London. As Rumford remarked in one of his essays,[11]

*I never view from a distance as I come into town the black cloud
which hangs over London without wishing to be able to compute the*

enormous number of caldrons of coal of which it is composed. For, could this be ascertained, I am persuaded, so striking a fact would awaken the curiosity and excite the astonishment of all ranks of the inhabitants and perhaps turn their minds to an object of economy to which they have hitherto paid little attention.

Rumford's solution to the problem was a crucial innovation that put a kind of ledge, or lip, at the back of the chimney just above the fireplace. Cold air coming down the chimney would hit this lip and be deflected into the stream of rising hot air from the fire to go up the chimney without interfering with the fire or getting into the room. As a result, clean air was drawn into the fire from the room, providing a steady draft that made it glow brightly—as Rumford realized, most of the heat that warms a room from such a fire comes from radiation, not convection. His later experiments also showed that dark objects radiate heat more effectively than shiny reflectors—good reflectors are poor radiators, and vice versa.[12]

In terms of the development of science, the key thing about Rumford's fireplaces is that they were designed on the basis of his theoretical understanding of heat and convection, not by trial and error. Science came first; technology followed. Rumford's design was a sensation, and has not been improved significantly to the present day. He claimed to have personally altered (or had altered at his direction?) five hundred fireplaces in fashionable houses in London, starting with the homes of Sir Joseph Banks and the Marquis of Salisbury, and was gently caricatured by James Gilray warming himself at one of his own fireplaces. His stoves also caught on, both for heating rooms and for cooking. A piece of doggerel that appeared in print at the time sums up Rumford's impact in London:

Lo, ev'ry parlour, drawing room I see,
Boasts of thy stoves and talks of *naught* but *thee.*
Yet, not *alone* my LADY and young MISSES,
The *cooks themselves* could smother thee with kisses!

All this brought Rumford a considerable income as he traveled around the country advising institutions of various kinds, and the wealthy, how to remodel stoves, fireplaces, and kitchens. And in Jane Austen's *Northanger Abbey*, published in 1817, her heroine's description of General Tilney's home includes her surprise at the fireplace, where "she had expected the ample width and ponderous carving of former times" but found it "contracted to a Rumford."

While Sally was being "polished" (with only limited success), in the spring of 1796 Rumford spent May and June in Dublin, then ruled from Britain, at the request of the Secretary of State for Ireland, Lord Pelham. He introduced the same kind of improvements in hospitals and poorhouses that he had developed in Bavaria, together with his ideas about kitchens and fireplaces. On his return to London, he supervised changes being made in the Foundling Hospital to enable it to provide a more efficient service, especially by reducing the costs of cooking food while improving its nutritional value. He also came up with a plan to use some of his by now considerable wealth to ensure that his name would be remembered by future generations. In November 1795 he had already been able to send $5,000 to his mother directly, now that he had no worries about his wife learning of his whereabouts. In July 1796 he offered the Royal Society in London and the American Academy of Arts and Sciences in Boston £1,000 each (equivalent to $5,000 at the time) as capital, from which the interest should be used to provide prizes for the invention of heating or lighting devices that would "tend most to promote the good of mankind." Recipients would also receive a medal, the Rumford Medal. The proposal wasn't greeted with quite the warmth Rumford might have expected in London, because he made it clear to the Royal Society that it would be rather nice if the first Rumford Medal were awarded to . . . Count Rumford. Partly because of this, the fund was not established and the first medal awarded (to Rumford) until 1802; they are still being awarded, just as he hoped.[13] But the delay was also a result of a dramatic change in Rumford's circumstances in the summer of 1796.

While Rumford and Sally had been settling in in England, the European wars had been continuing. France was engaged on several fronts, with the main action now in Italy, where a young Napoleon Bonaparte was making his name fighting the Austrians. But farther north, a French army was approaching Bavaria from the west, and an Austrian army was approaching from the north. Although Bavaria was desperately trying to stay neutral, it looked as if, whether the Bavarians liked it or not, the two armies would clash around Munich. The old elector currently held the upper hand in the government of Bavaria, having, in spite of the attentions of his young bride, outlived many of his political opponents. The Duke of Zweibrücken, who would have been his heir, was one of them, and had now been succeeded by his brother Maximilian, who had originally introduced Rumford to the elector. The old duke had been a vigorous proponent of resistance to Austria and other superpowers, but the new duke shared Rumford's preference for a policy of appeasement and cooperation. But although he was now largely unopposed in Munich, Carl Theodor was terrified and planning to leave as soon as possible. There was nobody in Bavaria competent to handle the situation (it is only a slight exaggeration to say that, as far as government was concerned, there was nobody in Bavaria competent)—so Carl Theodor called on Rumford, who had already exceeded his six months' "leave," to return at once and sort things out. The "invitation" was accompanied by promises of a friendly welcome from the present government, The subtext, not for the first time, was that if he failed to sort things out the resulting mess could be blamed on the foreigner.

Rumford could have ignored the plea; there was no way the elector could force him to return. But, supremely confident in his own abilities, and perhaps seeing an opportunity for further advancement, in spite of his comfortable position in London Rumford set out for Bavaria, taking Sally with him as well as several servants and a thoroughbred horse as a gift for Countess Nogarola. It may not seem an ideal entourage with which to enter a war zone, but wars were very different then, and Rumford wasn't your average traveler. And the war would lead directly to Rumford's greatest scientific achievement.

Rumford and his entourage sailed from Yarmouth on July 24, 1796. With various armies on the march and fighting here and there, they had to take a circuitous route through Prussia (which was neutral at the time),

99

then south through Saxony to Regensburg and on to Munich along difficult roads, staying in uncomfortable inns. The highlight for Rumford came when one of his lady friends, the Baroness Kalb, met up with them at one stop and stayed overnight; she "surprised us most agreeably," Rumford told Lady Palmerston.

The journey took three weeks, and when he arrived in Munich Rumford found the place in chaos. Valuables and art treasures were being shipped out for safekeeping, and on August 22, the elector himself fled, leaving a Regency Council in charge. And yet, after having been summoned back from Britain because of the crisis, Rumford was given no official position, but merely asked to act as the elector's personal representative in Munich—his eyes and ears in the city. The balance of power had shifted yet again, and Rumford was not the man the majority of those with influence wanted running anything. That changed when the situation deteriorated further, and they needed a scapegoat.

In the present phase of the European conflict, France was at war with Austria, and Bavaria was officially neutral. But Bavaria was part of the Holy Roman Empire, and so owed at least technical allegiance to Austria, although in fact there was no love lost between the Austrians and the Bavarians. When a French force moved toward Munich from the west, the Austrians moved an army south to stop them, and expected to be given a free passage through Munich to fight their enemies. But the commander of the Bavarian forces, Count Morawitzky (who was, naturally, a member of the Regency Council), closed the gates to the city and told the Austrians to go around it, using what Rumford describes as "language rather too gross and insulting to be borne with patience by the General of a formidable Army." That general, La Tour, came into the city to negotiate, where the situation was made worse. He was met by a detachment of cavalry with drawn swords, and escorted like a prisoner rather than an honored guest. The upshot was that the Austrian army, complete with their cannon, camped on the high ground overlooking the town, ready to meet the French but also effectively putting the city under siege. A way of placating the Austrians had to be found as a matter of urgency, and the council hit on the wheeze of sacking Morawitzky and putting Rumford in charge of the army and the defense of the city, with the title "Regency Commandant." They expected a disaster, for which they could then blame the foreigner who was the elector's favorite, with any luck getting rid of both Rumford and the elector. They reckoned without Rumford's guile.

This was a situation tailor made for the sometime spy, a person for whom the term "self-made man" might have been invented. He rode out to the Austrian camp, made profuse apologies for the conduct of his predecessor, and gave the general assurances that there was no need for his troops to enter Munich, because the Bavarians would themselves defend the city against the French. Messages were then sent to the French (less publicly) assuring them that there was no need for them to enter Munich, because the Austrians weren't there. The French advance forces got as close as the boundary of the English Garden, where a contingent camped between August 29 and September 11, but they retreated out of range when they came under cannon fire from the Austrians. The city was never attacked, but it was cut off. Rumford's greatest achievement as commandant, even more than his diplomacy, was that during the siege he kept the population, swelled by about twelve thousand troops, fed.

During the siege, Rumford maintained strict rationing of food and firewood, and designed and had built portable kitchens that could be carried on a single cart but could be used to cook for a thousand people. Until this time, soldiers had cooked for themselves over open fires; Rumford introduced the idea of centralized feeding of large groups of soldiers, applying it to civilians as well during the siege. The siege also gave him the opportunity to revive one of his civic projects. Before he had left on his latest visit to Britain, he had come up with the idea of building a grand boulevard around the city, to separate the urban areas from the countryside. While he was away, the city authorities had deliberately constructed buildings on the line of this proposed boulevard, to block his scheme. During the siege, Rumford claimed that these buildings were in the way of the defending army, and had them pulled down. After the crisis was over, and his prestige was back to its highest level, Rumford duly got his boulevard.

The crisis lasted only a few weeks, because the French withdrew when another of their armies suffered a defeat farther to the south, and the Austrians then moved back toward Vienna.[14] Carl Theodor returned on October 7, and by the end of October Rumford, hailed as the hero of the hour and savior of the city, was able to relinquish his power as commandant as the elector took up the reins. His reward was the post of commandant of the Bavarian police, the appointment of his daughter Sally (now to be formally known as Sarah) to the honorary title of countess, and the stipulation that the yearly pension that Rumford was receiving from Bavaria, equivalent to about £400 a year, would be split between him and his daughter and paid to them for life, wherever they might choose to live. This was no small gesture, because it's clear from his correspondence that Rumford hankered after a new life as a scientist, either in London or America; but for the time being he was honor bound to stay in Munich, where his social standing ensured that this wasn't much of a hardship. And his duties there soon gave rise to his most famous, and important, scientific contribution—an insight into the nature of heat, disproving the then popular idea that heat was a kind of fluid, called caloric. As his scientific masterpiece, we gave it the attention it deserves in the Prologue, where you can review it in its historical context.

With ideas like this buzzing around his head—and Rumford carried out many other experiments in Munich that are only less worthy of mention in comparison with his groundbreaking study of heat produced by friction—it's hardly surprising that he was eager to leave this scientific backwater and find a base where his talent would get the recognition it deserved. With nothing more that he could achieve in Munich, this was clearly the next "opportunity of advancement." Besides, things were getting somewhat uncomfortable in Bavaria. On a personal level, the relationship with Sally (now Sarah, Countess Rumford) had been damaged when she discovered that her father had another daughter.

The revelation came at a party for Rumford's forty-fourth birthday, on March 26, 1797. This was a lavish affair for which Sally had been helping Countess Nogarola to prepare for three weeks. Many children were present, and Sally tells us in the memoir included in the book by Ellis how the realization that she had a sister dawned on her when she noticed that a little eight-year-old girl called Sophy whose mother was Countess Baumgarten *had a more dignified part to act than any of us, being signalized out by my father (while the Countess, her children, and myself were barely noticed) as the object of great attention. . . . I applied to the Countess to know what it meant. She, not giving me a positive answer, smiling, said I was not to take notice that her sister, the Countess of Baumgarten, was not present. . . . This added to the mystery. . . . I returned with eagerness to my business of watching, and in consequence of it the truth was revealed to me. . . . The striking resemblance that existed between my father and the said Sophy put it beyond a doubt that I was no longer to consider myself an only child.*

In the spring and summer of 1797 Rumford was busy with experiments and writing up his scientific work ready for publication. The most important discovery he made at this time involved convection, and like so many scientific discoveries it happened by accident. Rumford was working with large thermometers filled with a variety of liquids, and one of them happened to have a little dust floating in it. After making some measurements, he put the thermometer in a window to cool down, where the dust motes caught the sunlight, and a little later when he glanced that way. he states:

I saw the whole mass of liquid in the tube in a most rapid motion, running swiftly in two opposite directions, up and down at the same time. . . . [O]n examining the spirits of wine with a lens, I found that the ascending current occupied the axis of the tube, and that it descended by the side of the tube.[15]

This was the first time that anyone had realized that convection currents, an understanding of which had been crucial to Rumford's fireplace and chimney designs, also occur in liquids.

In another series of experiments, aimed at measuring the effectiveness of water as an insulator of heat, Rumford was disconcerted to discover that hot water floated onto a layer of ice-cold water sank below the cold water, even though he expected the hotter liquid to be less dense and stay floating on top. But this time his friend Charles Blagden was able to explain what was going on. Blagden had been studying what he called "the expansion by cold" of water, and knew that water has a maximum density not at the freezing point but at a temperature of about 40 degrees Fahrenheit, 8 degrees above the freezing point. Curiously, at both higher and lower temperatures the water is less dense than it is at this critical temperature. As the hot water floating on top of the ice water in Rumford's experiment cooled, it reached the critical temperature and became dense enough to sink below the even colder water underneath. Heat was being carried downward by this water.[16]

A few years later, as we describe in chapter 9, these two discoveries would be linked in Rumford's explanation of a strange natural phenomenon. But in 1798, in his *Essay upon the Propagation of Heat in Fluids*,[17] he was already drawing attention to the peculiar behavior of water:

> *Though it is one of the most general laws of nature with which we are acquainted, that all bodies, solids as well as fluids, are condensed[18] by cold; yet, in regard to water, there appears to be a very remarkable exception to this law. Water, like all other known bodies, is indeed condensed by cold at every degree of temperature which is considerably higher than that of freezing, but its condensation, on parting with Heat, does not go on till it is changed to ice; but when in cooling its temperature has reached the 40th degree of Fahrenheit's scale, or eight degrees above freezing, it ceases to be further condensed; and on being cooled still farther, it actually expands, and continues to expand, as it goes on to lose more of its Heat, till at last it freezes; and at the moment when it becomes solid, and even after it has become solid, it expands still more, on growing colder.*

He saw this as striking evidence for the hand of God in providing us with a suitable home for life, because ice floating on top of water provides an insulating layer that keeps the water beneath relatively warm:

> *Had not Providence interfered in a manner which may well be considered as miraculous, all the fresh water within the polar circle must inevitably have been frozen to a very great depth in one winter, and*

every plant and tree destroyed; and it is more than probable that the regions of eternal frost would have spread on every side from the poles, and, advancing towards the equator, would have extended its dreary and solitary reign over a great part of what are now the most fertile and most inhabited climates of the world.

In 1797, in addition to carrying out experiments of this kind Rumford also found time for travel, sometimes with Sally and on one occasion with another of his close female friends, the Princess Taxis, a niece of George III's Queen Charlotte and an aunt of the future wife of Tsar Nicholas II. This socializing also gave rise to a conflict with Sally. Having already dismissed one suitor out of hand, he now seems to have been determined to nip any prospective romance in the bud. Rumford's aide de camp at this time was Count Taxis, a distant relative of the princess, whose gallantry and attentions made a deep impression on Rumford's daughter. The mother of Countess Nogarola seems to have encouraged the possibility of a liaison, but as soon as Rumford got wind of the situation he arranged for the regiment of Count Taxis to be posted away from Munich. Taxis later died, along with thousands of Bavarians, as a member of Napoleon's army in Bonaparte's Russian campaign.

At a professional level, as memories of the siege of 1796 faded and the aging elector's grip on power weakened once again, the future didn't exactly look encouraging. By 1798, Bavaria was being infected by the revolutionary fervor spreading from France, and in February Rumford wrote to Lady Palmerston that there had been "alarming accounts of popular disturbances and other symptoms of revolutionary Phrenzy." As he was still minister of police, Rumford was put in charge of the government for the duration of the emergency, but as things soon calmed down he never had to take any drastic action. This brief return to a position of real power did, however, stir the resentment of his enemies at court, and the elector was not getting any younger. Carl Theodor had also signed a "secret" peace treaty with France, now ruled by the Directory, in which France guaranteed the continuation of the Bavarian system of aristocratic rule. This was not secret enough to escape the notice of Vienna, which was infuriated. Rumford was regarded by Vienna an enemy of Austria, not least because after the siege of Munich he had proposed raising a special army corps to make Bavaria more independent of Austria, and suggested an alliance with the Prussians. Austria had threatened war if the plan were carried out, so it was dropped. But getting rid of Rumford now would help to soothe the feathers ruffled by the latest insult.

So the elector and Rumford hit upon the plan (probably at Rumford's suggestion) of sending him to London as Bavaria's minister plenipotentiary to the court of St. James—in other words, the Bavarian ambassador. The only problem was, the elector didn't clear this with King George III, who had never liked Rumford and took great exception to the idea that a British subject (still technically an officer in the British army!) could be the representative in London of a foreign power. The king refused to accept the appointment, and the affair put a serious strain on relations between Britain and Bavaria. But Rumford and Sally had already arrived in London, on September 19, 1798, before he discovered that he was, at least at the court of St. James, persona non grata. It was time to take stock, and reinvent himself once more, having made his greatest direct contribution to science.

CHAPTER 7

Looking to the Future

THE BRITISH WERE SO EAGER TO PREEMPT ANY POSSIBILITY OF RUM-ford being accepted as the representative of Bavaria that almost as soon as he arrived at the Royal Hotel in London George Canning, who was then undersecretary of state for foreign affairs and later became prime minister, called on him with letters formally rejecting the appointment. But they allowed Rumford to save face. They had already written to their representative in Munich, Arthur Paget, pointing out that "the circumstance of Count Rumford having heretofore filled a confidential situation (that of Under-Secretary of State in the American Department) under his Majesty's Government, makes the appointment in his person peculiarly improper and objectionable."[1] But rather than asking Paget to convey this to the elector and formally advising Carl Theodor that Rumford was unacceptable, they let Rumford himself write to Munich saying that "my health is so deranged that for the moment it is absolutely impossible for me to undertake any public affairs at all," and resign the post that he had not actually taken up.[2]

For a few weeks Rumford fell into a gloomy depression, avoided society, and apparently took to drinking "large quantities of strong Burton ale."[3] But as always he refused to be overcome by a setback, and on October 27 he had recovered enough to write to Lady Palmerston, "I am, on the whole, not sorry for all that has happened to me within the last two or three months. I am handsomely out of a bad scrape. All my private affairs are wound up, and I am now a free independent Citizen of the world." In fact, part of the reason for his change of mood was that far from being free and independent, he was busily working behind the scenes on behalf of the elector. The British had become concerned at the feeble response of their ally Bavaria to the growing threat from France, and Rumford was able to use his negotiating skills to obtain financial support for Bavaria from Britain, in return for a promise to increase the Bavarian army to twenty thousand men in support of British influence on the continent—although his role was not widely acknowledged at the time.

With this out of the way, Rumford renewed his interest in kitchens, studying those at the Foundling Hospital, and in heat, visiting the astronomer William Herschel at Slough to discuss experiments with him. But for several months his principal preoccupation seems to have been planning a return to America. Rumford was now forty-five, he thought he had severed his ties to mainland Europe, and he had not exactly been welcomed with open arms on his return to England. It was natural that he should look somewhat nostalgically at the possibility of a return to the land of his youth. On September 28, 1798, he wrote to Loammi Baldwin setting out his somewhat rose-tinted vision of what the future might hold. "It is," he said,

> *my fixed intention to pay a visit to my friends in America as soon as ever it shall be in my power. . . . I have even a scheme for forming for myself a little quiet retreat in that country, to which I can retire at some future period and spend the evening of my life. . . . I shall not want anything magnificent. From forty to one hundred acres of good land, with wood and water belonging to it, if possible in a retired situation, from one to four miles from Cambridge.*

This idea seems to have quickly crystallized into something more definite, because in a letter to the American secretary of state, on December 8 Rufus King, his man in London, wrote that Count Rumford

> *proposes to establish himself at or near Cambridge. . . . [H]is knowledge, particularly in the military department, may be of great use to us. The Count is well acquainted with and has had much experience in the establishment of cannon foundaries; that which he established in*

Bavaria is spoken of in very high terms, as well as certain improvements that he has introduced in the mounting of flying artillery.

The "flying artillery" was a form of light cannon, designed by Rumford, that could be transported rapidly and put into action quickly. The young American republic lacked expertise in the manufacture of cannon in general and this kind of artillery in particular, and the prospect of tapping into Rumford's knowledge was highly attractive. Just at this time, in February 1799, Rumford's European ties were further weakened, when Carl Theodor died and was succeeded by Maximilian Joseph, the nephew who had provided Rumford's original introduction to the Bavarian court. Although the new elector confirmed Rumford's pension as a count, he also relieved him of all military duties and obligations.

The following month, in a letter to King written on March 13, 1799, Rumford mentioned a quarter-size model of the field gun, which he was having packed up and shipped to America, and offered to send all his "military books, plans, drawings, and models" as well. He also referred to "a conversation we had at your house on the great importance to the United States of the speedy establishment of a military school or academy." Discussions progressed so well that on September 8 King wrote that he had received orders from his government "to invite you in its name to return and reside among us, and to propose you to enter into the American service." He continued:

In the course of the last year we have made provision for the institution of a Military Academy, and we wish to commit its formation to your experience. . . . In addition to the Superintendence of the Military Academy, I am authorized to offer to you the appointment of Inspector-General of the Artillery of the United States, and we shall, moreover, be disposed to give to you such rank and emoluments, consistent with existing provisions . . . as would be likely to afford you satisfaction.

If Rumford had taken up the offer, he could have been the founding head of the academy that became West Point. But by then his situation in England had changed, and he had become involved in another project, the one that would become his lasting legacy.

An early sign of which way the wind was blowing came in a letter to Baldwin written on March 14, 1799, in which Rumford mentioned his disappointment at not being able to visit America that year, and enclosed "a small pamphlet which . . . will acquaint you with the reasons." That pamphlet was the prospectus for what became the Royal Institution (RI); but it had its genesis in discussions Rumford had had in 1795, on his previous visit to England, with Sir Thomas Bernard. Bernard's father had been the governor of Massachusetts between 1760 and 1769, and Thomas had been educated at Harvard, but married a wealthy heiress and became a philanthropist who had set up several institutions for the poor and needy, including a school for the blind, an institute for the protection of "climbing boys"—children sent up chimneys to clean them—and the Foundling Hospital. Bernard was naturally interested in the success of Rumford's workhouses and public kitchens in Munich, and Rumford had sent him a proposal for a similar establishment in London in a document dated January 1, 1796.[4] Rumford's proposal was not just for "an establishment for feeding and giving employment to the poor," but also what he called "a grand repository" of useful mechanical inventions, partly for the education of the public, but also "containing the name of the inventor, the place where the article may be bought, and the price of it." Bernard organized a Society for Bettering the Conditions and Increasing the Comfort of the Poor, with objectives along the lines of the first part of Rumford's proposal, but ignoring the second part. Over the next few years, in correspondence with Bernard, Rumford tried to get the aims of the society extended to include what he called a House of Industry, but got nowhere. In 1799, after failing one more time to change the mind of the society, it was amicably agreed that he should start his own institution.

"The gentlemen of the Committee agreed with me entirely," wrote Rumford in March 1799, "in the opinion I had taken the liberty to express, that the Institution which it was proposed to form would be too conspicuous, and too interesting and important, to be made an *appendix* to any other existing establishment." So he published a pamphlet titled "Proposals for Forming by Subscription, in the Metropolis of the British

Empire, a Public Institution for Diffusing the Knowledge and Facilitating the General Introduction of Useful Mechanical Inventions and Improvements, and for Teaching by Courses of Philosophical Lectures and Experiments, the Application of Science to the Common Purposes of Life." This was the document enclosed with the letter to Baldwin explaining why he no longer planned an immediate visit to America. Establishing his institution became Rumford's driving passion for the next few years, and as Sally went back to America in August 1799, he was able to pursue it without distraction.

Rumford's skill at getting his own way with things is highlighted by the way he handled a delicate situation involving his daughter and his best male friend around this time. Sometime during the months before their return to England, Sally had received a proposal of marriage from Blagden—or, rather, Blagden had written to Rumford asking for permission to propose. Sally describes Blagden as "not so old as my father, but not young."[5] He had actually been born in 1748, so he was five years older than Rumford, who firmly opposed the match. She describes in her memoir how, without mentioning the letter, from time to time he casually repeated anecdotes about Blagden "not of a nature to enchant a young person," so that when news of the proposal was given to her she "was shocked that the thing should be mentioned," and turned it down flat. This "did not prevent all three of us being excellent friends when we met again," but there was nothing to keep her in London. Sally, now twenty-five, arrived in Boston on October 10, 1799, and was met by Baldwin, who escorted her home. Ellis tells us that on New Year's Day 1800 a ball was held at Woburn in her honor, where she appeared "in one of her court dresses, of blue satin." Baldwin continued to act as Rumford's agent handling money the count sent over for his daughter and mother, who was now a widow for the second time, her husband having died in August.

Meanwhile, Rumford's plans had progressed rapidly. His proposal for his new institution came, once again, in two parts; and once again things did not turn out the way he had planned. One component of the institute was to be a kind of museum of useful objects, including full-scale replicas of things like fireplaces and kitchens (featuring, of course, his own inventions), along with working scale models of things like steam engines. But the second objective of the institution was to be "TEACHING THE APPLICATIONS OF SCIENCE to the USEFUL PURPOSES OF LIFE," with "a lecture-room . . . fitted up for philosophical lectures and experiments and a complete LABORATORY and PHILOSOPHICAL APPARATUS, with the necessary instruments . . . for making *chemical* and other *philosophical experiments*."[6]

Rumford's prestige was so great that fifty-eight wealthy subscribers, contributing 50 guineas each, signed up for the scheme even before the first meeting, held at Joseph Banks's house on March 7, 1799, to formalize the plans and elect managers for the project. They included Rumford, Banks (then president of the Royal Society), and Bernard. A sum of £5,000 was soon raised. With breathtaking speed, the managers bought a house at 21 Albermarle Street, costing all but £500 of the initial subscription; hired an architect, Thomas Webster, to convert it; and persuaded George III to become Patron of what thereby became the RI.[7] Money kept pouring in, as much as £30,000, even though Britain was embroiled in the European wars. It was even agreed that ladies should be admitted as "proprieters and subscribers," although of course they "will not be called upon to take part in the management" of the institution. The snag was, it quickly became clear that what the wealthy subscribers thought they had signed up for and what Rumford wanted were two different kettles of fish.

Rumford hoped to use the institution to better the poor through education and training. This approach is highlighted by his plans for Webster, the twenty-six-year-old architect. Webster already had experience running a school for mechanics, and Rumford intended that he could continue this work within the RI, teaching things like principles of mechanics and technical drawing, so that people could better themselves. The thought horrified the backers of the RI, already alarmed by the fear that the "infection" of the French Revolution might spread across the English Channel, who thought that people should know their place in society and stay there. By contrast, Webster later wrote that he " did not think a little learning was a dangerous thing *if judiciously bestowed*" and that his idea was not to "force them like hot-bed plants out of the sphere in which they are so useful." A start was made on a School for Mechanics, but Webster's ambitions were soon frustrated, although the young man remained as architect and general manager in charge of the changes being made to the RI's home.

All of the frantic activity getting the RI off the ground took its toll on Rumford's health—he was probably suffering from stomach ulcers—and once Sally had left for America he visited Lady Palmerston in Hampshire and took a tour of Britain, leaving the running of the RI in other hands from September 14, 1799, to February 3, 1800. Shortly before he left, Dr. Thomas Garnett was appointed as the institution's first professor of natural philosophy and chemistry and scientific secretary, and Webster was formally appointed as clerk of the works. Even while "resting" Rumford was not idle. He wrote a long essay detailing his work on kitchens and fireplaces, indulged in extensive correspondence in which among other things he fretted about the neglect of his projects in Munich by the new regime there, and produced a new "Prospectus of the Royal Institution of Great Britain," which was essentially a public relations exercise to encourage support from the kind of people who had been alarmed at the prospect of educating the masses above their station. Instead of mentioning a school for mechanics, it talks rather of the lecture rooms and laboratories where "men of the first eminence in science will be engaged to officiate." This change of emphasis was also a response to the complete failure of Rumford's plan for an exhibition of working examples of new machines. Boulton and Watt, the leading manufacturers of steam engines, flatly refused to supply machines and drawings that their rivals might copy; Matthew Boulton even initially turned down election as a proprietor of the RI, only accepting the honor after Rumford had departed. Copies of the new prospectus were widely distributed, including to colleges in the United States, where Rumford hoped that someone might follow his example.

When Rumford returned to the RI in February 1800, however, he found that his example wasn't being followed very well even there. Progress was going so slowly that he moved out of his house in Brompton Row and into 21 Albermarle Street to take personal charge of the works, 24/7. He also took personal charge of producing the first issue of the *Journal of the Royal Institution*, which should have been one of Garnett's jobs. Garnett was genuinely having difficulty getting the facilities he needed constructed and preparing his lectures for the first season of the RI, but the workaholic Rumford saw this as a feeble excuse and the relationship between the two men continued to deteriorate, showing the ruthless side of Rumford's character. The tension between keeping the subscribers happy and what Rumford really wanted built during the first year the RI was operating, and through no fault of his own Thomas Garnett was caught in the middle.

Garnett had trained as a physician, but became a successful lecturer, and in 1796 took up a post at the new Anderson's Institution in Glasgow. He combined lecturing with a successful medical practice, and seemed settled there; but on Christmas Day 1798, when Garnett was thirty-two, his wife died in childbirth, leaving him with the baby girl and another infant daughter. The offer of a professorship at the RI gave him an opportunity to make a new start away from distressing memories, but London was not what he had expected. He was not allowed to practice medicine to supplement his modest salary (£300 a year), and the rooms at the RI did not have facilities for him to keep his daughters with him, so they had to stay with relatives in Westmoreland. In spite of everything, he gave the first public lecture (in a temporary room) when the RI officially opened on March 4, 1800, and his course proved a huge success with the fashionistas who had a dilettante interest in science. This, although essential for the financial success of the RI, was a far cry from providing education for mechanics, and Rumford continued to snipe at Garnett, forcing him to make a public apology when Garnett mistakenly attributed a new discovery in electricity to French scientists rather than to Alessandro Volta. When Garnett completed his lecture series in June he left for the north to be with his daughters while preparing material for the next course, due to start in January 1801.[8] Rumford promptly fired Garnett's assistant, the indispensable "chemical operator" who carried out the demonstrations during the lectures; this was ostensibly as an economy measure, but it seems to have been an early shot in a campaign to force Garnett out. This antipathy was in spite of a contemporary report that although Garnett's northern accent

rendered his voice somewhat inharmonious to a London audience, his
modest and unaffected manner of delivering his opinions, his familiar
and at the same time elegant language rendered him the object of
almost universal kindness and approbation.

It was also Garnett who introduced the strict rule, still adhered to at the
RI, that "the lectures will always begin at a certain hour to a minute."

An insight into Rumford's character at this time comes from the
commentator "Peter Pindar" (the pen name of John Wolcot), who wrote,[9]

Although a man may, like the count, possess extraordinary intellect,
and though a man may be the best judge of himself, nevertheless it is
indecorous to treat the opinion of others with contempt. The Count's
assertion is, "I never was yet in the wrong; I know everything."
Granted this to be true, the declaration nevertheless is arrogant and
supercilious.

Rumford was still suffering from the effects of overwork, but having
shown Garnett who was boss he was now satisfied that he had the upper
hand at the RI; with his protégé Webster in charge of the building works
and the season over, he went to Harrogate early in July for a course of
treatment at the baths. But being Rumford, he didn't just follow the
advice of his doctors on how best to benefit from the hot waters of
the natural springs at the spa, but experimented on himself to find out
which treatment was most effective. He changed the timing and length
of his baths, altered the timing of his meals, recorded how he felt during
these experiments, and (of course) wrote everything up as an essay titled
"Observations Concerning the Salubrity of Warm Bathing and the Principles on Which Warm Baths Should Be Constructed," finishing with
designs for steam baths ranging from "a scale of magnificence and refine-
ment" to "a less expensive and more modest plan." He would surely have
been delighted with the magnificent Victorian Turkish Baths opened in
Harrogate in 1897, and still in use today. According to his essay, Rumford
found that the best benefit was gained by taking a bath at a temperature
of 96 or 97 degrees Fahrenheit for half an hour two hours before dinner.

This increased his appetite, improved digestion, raised his spirits and strength, and made him less sensitive to cold.

It is a moot point, however, how much Rumford actually benefited from the "cure." As he wrote to Pictet,[10]

> *The waters have certainly been of much service to me, though I do not think it likely that they will radically cure my complaint. Idleness and amusement would be the most efficacious remedy; but I cannot be idle, nor can I amuse myself with moderation. The ardour of my mind is so ungovernable that every object that interests me engages my whole attention, and is pursued with a degree of indefatigable zeal which approaches to madness. It is no wonder that my health should be impaired by such continual excesses.*

This self-analysis provides the best insight we have into Rumford's character and the secret of his success, and it is appropriate that he should have expressed it so clearly himself.

From Harrogate, Rumford made his way to Edinburgh, where as usual his idea of a holiday involved carrying out experiments, this time in collaboration with members of the university but not producing any significant results, and discussing schemes to improve the lot of the poor. His advice to Heriot's Hospital enabled them to produce an improved heating and cooking system, which made it easier to prepare food at reduced cost. Rumford was made a member of the Royal Society of Edinburgh and the Scottish Royal College of Physicians, as well as a member of the Society of Scotland for Bettering the Conditions of the Poor. By November, however, he was back in London overseeing preparations for the completion of the building works at the RI and the next season of lectures starting in January 1801. These would be held in the superb new lecture hall at 21 Albermarle Street, designed by Webster but echoing the design of the one at Anderson's Institution. Other features of the RI, including the library, were also laid out along the same lines as in the Glasgow Institution, indicating Garnett's input into the planning. The lecture room has excellent acoustics (as we know from personal experience speaking there) and remains an almost original feature of the RI.

One of the original features that has been lost, however, is the pioneering steam heating system that Rumford had installed, with a large copper pipe running under the seats. This seems to have been highly effective, but at some point in the nineteenth century it fell out of use and was forgotten.

Early in 1801, Rumford began to turn the screws on Garnett, with results that proved disastrous for Garnett but serendipitously ensured the success of the RI. Rumford found an excuse he was obviously looking for when Garnett published the outlines for his next two courses of lectures in a pair of pamphlets, without consulting Rumford. His response was to establish a committee that existed solely to oversee the material for future lecture series. There were only three members of the committee—Rumford, Banks, and the great physicist Henry Cavendish, who was so reclusive that although he made many significant discoveries he seldom published his results, which often led other people to discover them independently and get the credit.[11] At a meeting held on February 2, 1801, the managers of the RI formally voted the committee into existence, resolving that "no syllabus of lectures . . . at the Royal Institution, be published by any person or persons without the permission of the aforesaid committee." Two weeks later, at their next meeting, they voted to hire a certain Humphry Davy as assistant lecturer in chemistry, and offered Davy one of the rooms up to then occupied by Garnett, with a salary of 100 guineas a year, plus "Coals and candles." The managers also repeatedly refused to increase Garnett's salary, although he had been promised incremental increases when he took up the post. The writing on the wall was clear, but Garnett hung on until June 1, when Davy was promoted to lecturer in chemistry and given a raise in salary. Garnett, as Rumford clearly intended, resigned.

The rest of Garnett's story can quickly be told. He moved to Great Marlborough Street, brought his family to London, and began practicing as a doctor again while starting a series of lectures on science and natural philosophy. In June 1802, he caught typhus from one of his patients, and died on June 28, just over a year after resigning from his post at the RI. The children were left destitute, but his executors arranged for the publication of some of his lectures, which raised nearly 2,000 guineas for them by subscription. The managers of the RI contributed £50.

Davy fared rather better. Never was a round peg better fitted for a round hole. When he came to the RI Davy was only twenty-two, a dark, handsome, and eloquent young man from Cornwall, who had been drawn to Rumford's attention by one of the founding subscribers to the RI, one Thomas Underwood. It may be that Rumford saw something of himself in Davy, because the Cornishman's early life had echoes of that of Benjamin Thompson; it also shows how tight-knit the scientific community of Britain was in those days. Davy had been born on December 17, 1778, the son of a struggling farmer. When his father died in 1794, Davy became apprenticed to an apothecary, and embarked on a program of self-education very similar to that of Thompson at the same age. He might have gone on to become a doctor, but not long before his nineteenth birthday he read Lavoisier's book *Traité Elémentaire* (in French, a language he had learned from a priest who had fled from revolutionary France) and fell in love with chemistry.

At that time, Gregory Watt, the son of James Watt of steam engine fame, was living as a lodger in the Davy household, and helped Davy develop his interest in chemistry during the winter of 1797–1798. Through the Watts, Davy got a job in October 1798 as assistant to Thomas Beddoes, of Bristol, a physician and chemist who had studied under Joseph Black in Edinburgh. In Bristol, Davy carried out experiments with nitrous oxide, known as "laughing gas" for its intoxicating effect on people. By accident, while suffering a toothache on the day of one of these experiments, he discovered that it also dulled the sensation of pain, and even suggested that it might be used as an anesthetic during operations, but this suggestion was not followed up at the time. Davy also carried out experiments with other gases, and wrote his work up in a book published in 1800, before turning his attention to the study of electricity. It was against this background that he was recruited by Rumford, for that initial salary of 100 guineas per year and free accommodation at Albermarle Street. But having made what he saw as a mistake in appointing Garnett sight unseen on the basis of his reputation, Rumford took great care to check Davy out before he was offered the post. He was interviewed several times, both by Rumford alone and by the committee he had devised to oversee the syllabus, and even gave a trial lecture in front of Rumford as a kind of audition, before being offered the job. He took to it like the proverbial duck to water.

Although he was officially hired as a chemist, the boundaries between the disciplines were loose in those days and as well as lecturing on "pneumatic chemistry," the work that had drawn him to the attention of the scientific world, in the spring of 1801 Davy also gave a course on electricity ("galvanism"). Rumford was actively involved in this work, and when Davy communicated his first paper to the Royal Society in June it described the invention of a new "galvanic apparatus," a wet-cell battery "constructed after the ideas of Count Rumford." This was the beginning of Davy's greatest contribution to science, which came to fruition after Rumford had left London, and which we describe in the coda.

Davy was also encouraged to revive Rumford's idea of practical lectures for working men, including techniques of tanning leather, but unlike the work on electricity these did not long survive Rumford's departure. This disengagement was gradual, but it began in the summer of 1801 when, after Garnett's departure, and at Banks's suggestion, Thomas Young was appointed as professor of natural philosophy at the RI and Rumford moved out of 21 Albermarle Street to make room for him. Where Garnett had been professor of natural philosophy and chemistry, Rumford's machinations had now provided the RI with two professors, one in each discipline. Unfortunately, although Young was a scientific genius, at the RI he was something of a square peg in a round hole.

Young was born to Quaker parents in 1773, and was a child prodigy who excelled at just about everything, from classical languages (he translated Shakespeare into Greek iambic verse when he was sixteen) to science; studied medicine; and became a Fellow of the Royal Society at the age of twenty-one, after publishing a paper on crystalline lenses. In 1796, Young passed his medical examinations in Germany, but when he returned to England the following year he found that in order to be a Fellow of the College of Physicians he had to spend two years studying (or at least in residence) at Cambridge or Oxford, regardless of his other qualifications. He chose Emmanuel College, in Cambridge. There, he stood out from his fellow students both because he was slightly older than most of them and because of his proficiency at whatever he chose to turn his mind to, gaining the nickname "Phenomenon Young." It was while he was in Cambridge that he began his study of light, which resulted in a series of three papers published by the Royal Society in 1801, 1802, and 1803, which established that light travels as a form of wave, overturning the "corpuscular" theory promoted by Isaac Newton, which had held sway for a hundred years.[12] This is now regarded as Young's greatest work, although at the time it was controversial. It was something of a coup when he accepted the engagement at the RI, for a salary of £300 per year. We have a little more to say about Young's contribution to the RI later; in spite of his brilliance he failed to appeal to the kind of audiences the institution needed for its financial success, which was a crucial consideration at the time. Bence Jones quotes a contemporary account that sums up the situation:

> *Dr. Young, whose profound knowledge of the subjects he taught no one will venture to question, lectured in the same theatre, and to an audience similarly constituted to that which was attracted by Davy, but he found the number of his attendants diminish daily, and for no other reason than that he adopted too severe and didactic a style.*

He was, it seems, better suited to lecturing in Oxford or Cambridge than to the dilettante audience at the RI. His role there came to an end in July 1803.

Back in the summer of 1801, Rumford had returned to his house in Brompton Row, where he installed some of the home improvements that he had been unable to persuade the managers of the RI to display as "models." These included double-glazed windows, a folding bed, and many of his other domestic inventions, which were described by Pictet after a visit to Rumford that year. "Everything," Pictet tells us, "has been carried out to the highest degree of economy and perfection. . . . The house is equipped with the most perfect simplicity and the most complete order."

With the RI now running more or less under its own steam, Rumford's own thoughts turned once again to the future. The idea of a visit—perhaps even a permanent relocation—to America remained a possibility, but the more pressing need was to travel to Munich to meet the new elector, Maximilian Joseph, and find out how his status there stood. This was a tricky issue, because although Carl Theodor had been a formal ally of the British, Maximilian Joseph had spent his military career in the French army, and Bavaria was now likely to become part of the French sphere of influence. This was potentially a particularly difficult situation for Rumford, as Britain and France were at war. Although the war had had little impact on London society, how would any change in Bavaria's allegiance affect a British colonel (albeit on half-pay) who was also a Bavarian count? On September 9, 1801, Rumford wrote to Lady Palmerston:

> *I go now to Munich . . . to pay my Court to my new Sovereign, and to settle with him, if possible, a reasonable plan for the rest of my life. I shall try hard to arrange matters so as to divide my time between England and Bavaria. My House at Brompton, and a Summer lodging at Munich, that is my scheme.*

But the scheme was overtaken by new personal developments before he got back to England.

Rumford traveled light when he left London at the end of September, determined to make only a flying visit before returning to oversee the establishment of the RI. He covered 828 miles in ten days, to receive a surprisingly warm welcome in Munich. On October 3 he wrote to Lady Palmerston:

> *I arrived in perfect health, and am now in the highest spirits. I found all my friends here well and everybody glad to see me. My reception from everybody has really been most flattering. I saw my Garden this afternoon, and found it in great beauty.*

He also saw his daughter Sophy Baumgarten, visited the princess of Taxis, and squeezed in a short trip to Mannheim to be with one of his lovers, Laura de Kalb. He wrote to Lady Palmerston that Sophy "promises to be a charming creature. She is very clever and very accomplished for a child of her age," which was then thirteen. But with everything in order in Bavaria, and the new elector so well disposed toward him that it was suggested that he might return to establish a new Academy of Arts and Sciences in Munich, Rumford stayed for only ten days before starting back to London. This time, however, although Britain and France were still at war, as a respected savant and a retired Bavarian general (glossing over the fact that he was also a retired British colonel) he obtained permission to travel via Paris, where Napoleon Bonaparte was now first consul. On this occasion he traveled at a leisurely pace and in exalted company. He wrote to Sally on the eve of his departure,t "I have the honour to accompany Prince George of Mecklenburg Strelitz, brother to the Queen of Prussia, as likewise the Princess of Taxis, a friend of mine." The princess, of course, was rather more than a "friend." The party arrived in Paris on October 25, where Rumford intended to stay for a week or so before proceeding to England. But the reception he received was so overwhelming that he ended up remaining there for two months, during which all his plans for the future changed.

We know a great deal about those two months, because Rumford kept a detailed diary of his visit, for the benefit of Lord Pelham, the British home secretary. This wasn't exactly spying, and it showed Napoleon in a good light, but the fact that a British citizen was staying in Paris reporting on the political scene there when Britain and France were at war highlights the way things have changed since then. The original diary has been lost, but Lady Palmerston made a copy of it that survives in the library of the University of Birmingham.[13] In addition, Rumford wrote letters to Banks and to Lady Palmerston, which also crossed safely from France to Britain, and which survive in the archives. One way or another, we know more detail about Rumford's activities during those two months in Paris than for any other two months of his life.

This was a time when France (at least among the higher levels of society) was undergoing a reaction against the excesses of the revolution, and Napoleon, although not yet an emperor, was surrounded by a glittering court of high-ranking officers, foreign diplomats, intellectuals, and (of course) beautiful women. As a "natural philosopher" of renown, Rumford was welcomed into Napoleon's inner circle, where he found that "the gratitude of all Ranks, to the first Consul, is unbounded." In Rumford's view, "[Napoleon] has certainly delivered this nation from the worst of all evils," and he wrote approvingly to Pelham (who would have shared his sentiments) that "you would be surprized at how seldom you meet with anything resembling Democracy—It is quite out of fashion—it is despised. . . . The word *Citoyen* is never hear'd in good company, and the word *Liberté* is become quite obsolete." It is easy to see why Rumford chose the British side in the American War of Independence. Rumford's assessment of Napoleon was entirely positive. He described Bonaparte as "a person endowed with very uncommon abilities," and said that "the more I see of him, and the more I consider the wonderful things he has done, and is doing, the more I am disposed to admire his genius."

The feeling was to some extent mutual. When Rumford was formally presented to Napoleon, the first consul seems to have shown a special interest in him, which enhanced Rumford's status in society. On November 11, he wrote to Banks that "my reception has been very flattering" and that he had met many eminent men of science and attended meetings of the National Institute, where on the most recent occasion

> the First Consul came in, and, fortunately for the complete gratification of my curiosity, he happened to come and seat himself very near me. One person only (Lagrange) was between us. He stayed about an hour—till the meeting was over. Volta read a memoir on Galvanism and explained his theory of the action of the voltaic pile or battery. His opinion is that all the appearances that are called galvanic are owing to the action of an electric fluid.

Rumford then explained to Banks that he had already been presented to Napoleon at his latest public audience, where

[I] was received by him with marked attention. He gave me to under-
stand that he knew my reputation very well, and intimated that
the French nation had adopted several of the improvements I had
recommended. A few minutes after I came home from the audience
I received a note from him, inviting me to come and dine with him
that day. The foreign ministers dined with him, but no other stranger
except myself was invited . . . a marked distinction.

Among the people Rumford met on this visit to Paris were the mathematical physicists Pierre-Simon de Laplace (who refined the laws of
celestial mechanics), Joseph Louis Lagrange (who had presided over the
metrication committee), Antoine Fourcroy (the first person to purify
urea, which he named), the notorious Charles Maurice de Talleyrand
(then minister of foreign affairs), a certain Joseph-Ignace Guillotine
(inventor of the eponymous execution device), the American revolutionary hero General Lafayette, and others who had been involved in the
American Revolution, now two decades in the past, on the opposite side
to Rumford. He discussed science, especially his ideas about heat, with
colleagues; promoted his ideas about kitchens; and was elected both as
a member of the Society for the Encouragement of National Industry
and to the National Institute (the Institut National de France, the revolutionary successor to the old Académie des Sciences) in the "class" for
achievements in political economy.

Part of the reason for Rumford's warm welcome in Paris was that
although a state of war formally existed between Britain and France,
both sides were edging toward a peace settlement. While Rumford was
in Paris, the British plenipotentiary Lord Cornwallis arrived for negotiations that eventually led to the Peace of Amiens, a treaty signed on
March 25, 1802 (but that only lasted until May 1803). Rumford was a
guest at a grand banquet held to mark the beginning of the discussions.

Rumford's other interests were not neglected, and his diary describes
visits to the women he spent time with, at the opera, at dinner, or on
visits to their homes. Fashionable women of the time stayed in their bed-
chambers for much of the day, wearing elegant bed gowns and waited on

hand and foot by servants. Rumford's diary entry for November 13, 1801, describes a typical visit to one of these ladies, Madame Laplace:

She is young (not 30) and very pretty. . . . [H]er bed dress and night Cap were récherchés and everything about her displayed the charms of refined luxury. She received me without the smallest degree of embar-rassment. . . . On coming away I made many excuses to Madame Laplace for having kept her in Bed till so late an hour. Indeed I felt quite ashamed of my indiscretion.

It cannot have been very indiscreet, because the Laplace's daughter, about eight years old at the time, was also present. In any case, we can probably take the last sentence with a pinch of salt, because it is just one of many such entries. But one of these encounters would change Rumford's life forever.

On November 19, 1801, he met an attractive widow, Marie Lavoisier, at a party. Two days later, he visited her at home, where he "sat with her an hour, and found her very lively, witty and pleasing in conversation." On December 2, "Mad. Lavoisier is a very cheerful friendly and good natured Woman and she is rich and independent." He continued:

Speaking of my philosophical pursuits and intended publications I observed that nothing amused me so much as making experiments but that it was tiresome to write an account of them. She said to me, "Venez vous établir ici et je veux être votre secrétaire, vous tra-vaillerez et moi j'écrirai."[14] That would be charming indeed was my answer.

On December 5, he wrote, "She is one of the cleverest woman I ever knew and is uncommonly well informed." From then on, he visited her every other day until December 13, when after having breakfasted with Madame Lavoisier he set out back to England. He was clearly smitten with Marie, and flattered by the attention he had received in Paris. Once again, it was time to move on and reinvent himself.

PART IV

THE FRENCH CONNECTION

CHAPTER 8

The Mother of Chemistry

THE WOMAN WHO WOULD CHANGE RUMFORD'S LIFE WAS BORN IN THE
Loire province on January 20, 1758, and named Marie-Anne Pierrette
Paulze.[1] Her father, Jacques, was a wealthy member of the upper ech-
elons of society, a lawyer, and a tax "farmer"—a member of the Ferme
Générale, which collected taxes on behalf of the government, receiving
a commission for the work and providing ample opportunity for less
scrupulous members to cream off additional funds. This was one of the
many injustices that would fuel the fervor of the French Revolution.
Marie's mother, Claudine, died when the child was three, and as the only
girl in the family (she had three brothers) she was sent to a convent to
be educated. This was no hardship, and one of the few places where a
bright girl could receive a good education; Marie seems to have been very
bright, and to have flourished in the environment. She left the convent
when she was twelve, and was intended to take over the running of her
widowed father's household. But everything changed in 1771, when she
was thirteen.

The Count of Amerval, a local bigwig and brother of the Baroness de
la Garde, was in financial difficulties and decided to solve his problems
by marrying money. He was fifty at the time, and decided that Marie
Paulze would be the ideal choice. When her father explained the situation to her, she was horrified. She described her prospective husband as
"fol d'ailleurs, agrest et dur, une espèce d'ogre" (a fool, an unfeeling rustic,
and an ogre).[2] The count and his sister put pressure on Jacques Paulze's

superior, who wrote to Jacques in an effort to force his (and Marie's) hand, but he replied,

> *M. d'Amerval is fifty, my daughter is only thirteen; he has not even 1,500 francs a year, and my daughter, although not wealthy, can at this moment bring twice as much to her husband. His character is not known to you, but that it cannot please either my daughter or you or myself, I am, indeed, well assured. My daughter has a decided objection to him; I will certainly not force her against her wishes.*

This was a dangerously principled stand to take, which threatened his career and position in society, but Jacques acted quickly to prevent any further approaches by the count to his daughter. He had a friend and colleague, the twenty-eight-year-old Antoine Lavoisier, whom he felt would make a good son-in-law. There is no record of how things were negotiated, but Marie obviously agreed that Antoine was a more desirable match than the count, and they were married on December 16, 1771, a month before her fourteenth birthday. The count's scheme was thwarted, there were no repercussions for Jacques, and the newlyweds seem to have genuinely come to love each other. Marie also soon began to collaborate with her husband in his chemical investigations.

Antoine-Laurent Lavoisier had been born in the Marais district of Paris on August 16, 1743. His father and his grandfather were both lawyers, and Antoine had a comfortable upbringing. He had one sister, two years younger than he was, but their mother died in 1748 and the family moved into the home of her widowed mother, where the unmarried aunt of the children, twenty-two at the time, looked after them. Antoine's sister, Marie, died in 1760; the following year, when he was eighteen, he began to study law at the University of Paris, graduating in 1763. But alongside his legal studies he had developed an interest in science, attending courses in astronomy, mathematics, botany, geology, and chemistry. Instead of practicing law, he spent three years as an assistant on a project to make a geological map of France, working in the field, collecting specimens and surveying. In 1766, Lavoisier's grandmother died, and left him enough money to live on in comfort, and in the same year he received a gold medal from the Royal Academy of Sciences for a study of how to improve street lighting. He was involved (as a partner, not mere assistant) in a survey of Alsace-Lorraine, and in 1768, at the age of only twenty-five, he was elected as a member of the Royal Academy of Sciences. Unlike its British counterpart, the French Academy was a professional institution whose members were paid salaries and carried out work of a scientific nature for the government, alongside any other work. Lavoisier thrived there, working on many useful projects, but in 1768 he made what turned out to be both a fortunate and a disastrous decision when he bought a one-third share in a tax farm. Lavoisier was a diligent and, as far as we can tell, honest "farmer" who collected taxes fairly and was well respected. It was through this work that Lavoisier became a colleague and friend of Jacques Paulze, and married Marie.

The marriage, although hastily arranged, was a good match, with the bonus that the couple actually liked each other. Marie brought with her a good dowry; Antoine, who was already independently wealthy, received an advance on his inheritance from his father, and later inherited from his aunt as well. In the ferme, over the years he first bought out one partner to become half-owner, then the remaining partner to become the sole fermier. He was rich enough to do anything he wanted, or nothing at all. He chose to study chemistry, but also to work for the good of society in a variety of roles, which we will not elaborate on here.

There is no doubt that Marie played an important part in Antoine Lavoisier's scientific work—they had no children and she devoted her married life to being his assistant, and perhaps more than his assistant. We shall never know how much she contributed to the ideas that have come down as his, although it does not seem that she was heavily involved in hands-on experimenting. We do know that she was taught chemistry by a colleague of Lavoisier, Jean Baptiste Bucquet; studied English and translated English works into French for Antoine; became a proficient artist (she was taught by the eminent painter Jacques Louis David) who engraved the plates for Antoine's book *Traité Élémentaire de Chimie* (1789) that was such an influence on Humphry Davy; and generally acted as Antoine's right-hand woman. Most of this work was carried out in their accommodation at the Paris Arsenal, where Antoine became a member of the Gunpowder Administration in 1775, after Louis XVI came to the throne.[3] This was a key post, recognizing his honesty and ability, in which he used his chemical knowledge to improve the product and his skill as an administrator to reform the management of the process. As a result, where France had been a net importer of gunpowder (a very dangerous situation in wartime) it became an exporter, among other things supplying the rebels in Britain's American colonies.

We get glimpses of Marie as Antoine's scientific collaborator in various letters and other writings. In 1775, when she was still only seventeen, one correspondent referred to her as Lavoisier's "philosophical wife." On September 13, 1787, Arthur Young, a British agricultural economist who visited the Lavoisiers in Paris, noted in his diary:

> *To M. Lavoisier by appointment.*
>
> *Madame Lavoisier, a lively, sensible, scientific lady, had prepared a déjeuné Anglois [dejeuner anglais] of tea and coffee, but her conversation on Mr. Kirwan's "Essay on Phlogiston" which she is translating from the English, and on other subjects which a woman of understanding that works with her husband in his laboratory knows how to adorn, was the best repast.*

And Gouverneur Morris wrote in his diary on June 8, 1789:

> *Dine with Mr. de Lavoisier. . . . Madame appears to be an agreeable woman. She is tolerably handsome, but from her manner it would seem that she thinks her forte is the understanding rather than her person.*

As this indicates, Antoine and Marie mingled with society in Paris, and hosted gatherings of their own. The people they met included foreign thinkers such as Benjamin Franklin, Joseph Priestley, and James Watt. And all the time "she proved an indefatigable promoter of the 'new chemistry' and her husband's renown."[4]

Her husband's renown today rests on three key contributions that he made to chemistry. Lavoisier did not make any significant discoveries himself, but on two crucial occasions followed through on discoveries made but not fully understood by others, explaining what was going on and changing the way people thought about the way substances interact. His third contribution, in which Marie played a significant part, was rationalizing the whole system of chemistry and bringing order to what had been a chaotic confusion.

At the time Marie married Antoine, it was thought that burning involved a substance, called phlogiston, being released from the thing that was burning. This was a natural explanation of why smoke and flames emerged from a burning object, but it didn't stand up to proper scientific investigation. If the idea was correct, you would expect substances to lose weight when they burned; but this was not the case. By 1771, it was known, partly from the work of Stephen Hales, an English clergyman and amateur natural philosopher, that phosphorus took up lots of air when burned, but nobody had explained this or measured it accurately. In 1772 Lavoisier carried out careful experiments, heating samples of sulfur and phosphorus in sealed glass containers using a powerful lens to focus the rays of the sun, and measuring the changes this caused. In a note read at the academy the following year, he said:

> I discovered that sulphur, in burning, far from losing weight, on the contrary gains it. . . . [F]rom a pound of sulphur one obtains much more than a pound of vitriolic acid [sulfuric acid]. . . . It is the same with phosphorus; this increase of weight arises from an abundant quantity of air that is fixed during the burning and combines with the vapours. This discovery, which I have established by experiments . . . has led me to think that what I have observed in the burning of sulphur and phosphorus may well take place in the case of substances that gain in weight in burning.

In 1774, the next clue to what was going on came from Joseph Priestley, another British clergyman/natural philosopher, when he visited Paris. This visit took place only a few weeks after Priestley had made his greatest discovery, as part of a much wider investigation that is not directly relevant here. Before Priestley's work, only two gases were known—air, and what was termed "fixed air," now called carbon dioxide. He had now used a lens to heat what was then known as the red calx of mercury in a glass vessel, and captured the gas that was released as the calx turned into a puddle of mercury. This gas had intriguing properties, and a lit candle plunged into it would flare up with unusual brightness. He later described how he told the Lavoisiers the news:[5]

> *I mentioned it at the table of Mr. Lavoisier when most of the philosophical people of the city were present, saying it was a kind of air in which a candle burned much better than in common air, but that I had not then given it any name. At this all the company, and Mr. and Mrs. Lavoisier as much as any, expressed great surprise*

At the time he met Lavoisier, Priestley was only beginning a long series of experiments that would reveal the properties of the gas (he called it "pure air") and its importance for maintaining life; this paralleled a lot of Lavoisier's work, which was inspired by Priestley's discovery, but they worked independently and we shall focus on Lavoisier here.[6] Starting in November 1774 he carried out his own experiments with red calx and in May 1775 published a paper stating that a calx is formed when a metal combines with the pure air discovered by Priestley. In 1779, he gave Priestley's "pure air" the name oxygen. He also followed up the significance of this pure air for life, and surmised that animals maintained their body heat by converting this pure air into fixed air in the same way that charcoal gives off heat by burning. But he didn't just speculate. In an approach that would have delighted Rumford, along with his fellow academician Pierre Laplace (and almost certainly with Marie's involvement), in the early 1780s he carried out some carefully crafted experiments involving a guinea pig to test the idea.

The guinea pig was put in a container surrounded by ice, inside a well-insulated larger container. The team measured how much ice was melted by the warmth of the animal in ten hours, then measured how much charcoal had to be burned to melt the same amount of ice. In separate experiments, they also measured how much "fixed air" the guinea pig breathed out in ten hours while resting, and found that within reasonable differences allowing for the imperfections of the experiment this was the same as the amount produced by burning enough charcoal to melt the same amount of ice as in the earlier experiment. They concluded that respiration "is therefore a combustion, admittedly very slow, but otherwise exactly similar to that of charcoal."

Lavoisier developed his theory of combustion over the next few years, and published his definitive rebuttal of the phlogiston model in the *Mémoires* of the academy in 1786. Although diehard proponents of the phlogiston model continued to debate the issue, what he said then has stood the test of time:

> 1. *There is true combustion, evolution of flame and light, only in so far as the combustible body is surrounded by and in contact with oxygen; combustion cannot take place in any other kind of air [gas] or in a vacuum, and burning bodies plunged into either of these are extinguished as if they had been plunged into water.*
> 2. *In every combustion there is an absorption of the air [gas] in which the combustion takes place; if this air is pure oxygen, it can be completely absorbed, if proper precautions are taken.*
> 3. *In every combustion there is an increase in weight in the body that is being burnt, and this increase is exactly equal to the weight of the air [gas] that has been absorbed.*
> 4. *In every combustion there is an evolution of heat and light.*

Some of the evidence for these conclusions came from Lavoisier's second great practical contribution to chemistry, which kicked off from a discovery made by the reclusive British genius Henry Cavendish. In 1766 Cavendish prepared a set of four papers describing his work with gases, but for some reason published only one of them, in the *Philosophical Transactions* of the Royal Society.[7] He had discovered that when acid is added to metals the mixture gives off another "air," but this time when the gas was collected in a container and it was tested with a flame, it exploded. He dubbed the gas "inflammable air," but then turned his attention to electricity, and only returned to the study of gases in the early 1780s, stimulated by Joseph Priestley's discovery that these explosions leave behind a residue of water. Among other things, Cavendish tested how violently different mixtures of inflammable air with ordinary air exploded, by sealing the gases in a copper or glass vessel and igniting them with an electric spark. Like other people who used this technique, he noticed that after the explosions the inner walls of the container were covered in a "dew" of water, but unlike those people's findings his careful measurements showed that there was no change in weight of the container as a result of the explosion. He published the results in 1784, concluding "though the experiment was repeated several times with different proportions of common and inflammable air, I could never perceive a loss of weight of more than one-fifth of a grain, and commonly none at all."

Cavendish's attempted explanation of what was going on was confused by his acceptance of the phlogiston model. But in June 1783, even before the results were published, Charles Blagden visited Paris where, among other things, he informed the Lavoisiers about Cavendish's latest work. Lavoisier lost no time following up the news, and immediately (on June 25, 1783) informed the academy that when inflammable air burned in ordinary air the result was "water in a very pure state." On November 12, he went further, declaring that water was not an element, because it could be "decomposed and recombined."

Lavoisier had taken things a crucial stage further first with experiments in which a stream of "inflammable air" (hydrogen) and a stream of "pure air" (oxygen) were brought together in a double nozzle arrangement and burned to produce water, and then with his explanation that this is another example of combustion—another nail in the coffin of the phlogiston model. It was also the death of the idea, going back to ancient times, that water was an element.

We know exactly how Antoine carried out his experiments, thanks to the accurate drawings Marie made of the apparatus, published in his papers and especially in his great book on chemistry, which inspired Humphry Davy to take up chemistry. These are so precise that the illustrations are one of the main sources of information about the equipment used by scientists in the late eighteenth century. The book itself, published in 1789, laid the foundations of modern chemistry as a scientific discipline, and its writing clearly owed much to Marie even if her name did not appear on the cover. Antoine Lavoisier has sometimes been called "the father of modern chemistry"; if so, Marie Lavoisier was undoubtedly the mother. Their joint work rationalized the nomenclature of chemistry, getting rid of old names such as "oil of vitriol," and gave the modern names to many substances, including oxygen, hydrogen, carbon, sulfur, phosphorus, other metals, and various oxides. The new rules introduced a logical system with, among other things, the "ic" ending for acids such as sulfuric acid and phosphoric acid, and set out, for example, that salts formed from acids would have an "ate" ending, as in magnesium sulfate. All this made it much easier for chemists to communicate information about their discoveries to one another. The Lavoisiers emphasized the importance of accurate measurement and experimentation, and stated clearly that matter is never created or destroyed in chemical reactions, but only converted from one form to another—the law of conservation of mass. And they defined, in the clearest way yet, an element as something that cannot be broken down into a simpler substance.

There was one huge blind spot in all of this. The list of elements in the book included caloric. Down the years, this has often been held up as a criticism of Lavoisier, but that is hardly fair. There can be little doubt that with his understanding of the scientific method and emphasis on accurate measurement he would have been convinced by Rumford's work in Munich that heat is a form of motion and that there is no such thing as caloric. But Antoine Lavoisier, although only forty-six in the year when his book was published, did not live to learn of Rumford's work, thanks to the political events that were set in motion in 1789, the year that *Traité Élémentaire de Chimie* was published.

In the early phase of the French Revolution, Antoine remained an important government adviser and administrator, working in a number of roles including the Gunpowder Administration, where his success was a key factor in ensuring that the French had sufficient high-quality gunpowder to meet the needs of the forces repelling foreign armies that attacked France in support of the old regime. From his letters, it is clear that Antoine was a reformer rather than a revolutionary, and would have favored a kind of parliamentary democracy like that in Britain, including a king. But very early on he appreciated the danger of the revolution going too far (as he would have thought) and on February 5, 1790, he wrote to Benjamin Franklin:

> *It would be well to give you news of our Revolution; we look upon it as over, and well and irrevocably completed; but there is still an aristocratic party, making some useless resistance and very weak. The democratic party is in the majority and is supported moreover by the educated, the philosophic, and the enlightened members of the nation. Moderate-minded people, who have kept cool heads during the general excitement, think that events have carried us too far, that it is unfortunate that we have been compelled to arm the people and to put weapons in the hands of every citizen. . . . We greatly regret your absence from France at this time; you would have been our guide and you would have marked out for us the limits beyond which we ought not to go.*

Those limits were not reached immediately, but with the rise of the Jacobins to power in 1793 the writing was on the wall. The Reign of Terror began, overseen by the blandly titled Committee of Public Safety, and Lavoisier may have hoped that his impeccable record of honesty and his continuing service to the government (he was then working on the Commission of Weights and Measures, among other responsibilities) would have kept him safe. But he had been a tax farmer, and the tax farmers were the most hated symbols of the old regime. It didn't matter that he had been an honest tax farmer. Along with eighteen of his colleagues (including Marie's father), he was arrested in November 1793 and charged with "incivisme" (counterrevolutionary activity), an offense that carried the death penalty. Marie lobbied the couple's influential friends to come forward in his defense, but nobody was brave enough to oppose the committee—a failure she never forgot or forgave. On May 7, 1794, the tax farmers, represented by just four lawyers who had been given only fifteen minutes to prepare for the defense of all the prisoners, were brought before a kangaroo court. The next day, May 8, they were formally found guilty and executed. At the scaffold, Jacques Paulze was third in line, and Antoine Lavoisier fourth; Antoine watched his father-in-law beheaded before it was his turn at the guillotine. Marie, now thirty-six, had lost her father and husband within a few minutes of each other, and was devastated. She was arrested herself (for no good reason) and imprisoned for sixty-five days, but released when the Terror ended in July with the fall of Robespierre.[8]

By then, she had also lost all her wealth, because the property of the tax farmers had been confiscated, but she was helped by a former servant. Fortunately for posterity, in due course she did recover much of Antoine's laboratory equipment and notebooks, and even some of the family property, but not all of the money, when he was posthumously rehabilitated eighteen months after his execution. As part of an attempt to rebuild her fortunes, she pressed an old family friend, Pierre-Samuel du Pont, to repay a large loan that he had received from the Lavoisiers years before. This was, to say the least, tactless, because du Pont had himself been imprisoned, narrowly avoided the guillotine, and was now nearly as broke as she was; it soured a relationship that had always been more than merely friendly, although historians disagree on just how much more.

Du Pont was some twenty years older than Marie, and they had become close friends in the 1780s; his teenage son, Eleuthère Irénée, had even been sent to study chemistry with Antoine Lavoisier. In 1795, after Antoine had been executed but before the financial complications, Pierre had even proposed to Marie, but been rejected. Surviving letters from du Pont to Marie are passionate enough to support the speculation that they began an affair while Antoine was still alive, taking advantage of his frequent absences on government business. On the other hand, du Pont seems to have favored an old-fashioned "courtly" style in his correspondence, expressing undying affection even to his male correspondents, and even in formal letters. But it is the end of their friendship that is relevant to the story of Marie and Rumford.

In 1799, the du Pont family moved to America, where they founded what became by 2018 a company with total revenue of $86 billion, and in 2019 was ranked number 35 on the Fortune 500 list of the largest US public corporations. All based ultimately on what Pierre's son had learned from Antoine Lavoisier. Shortly before they left, Pierre wrote a letter to

Marie that, whatever his relationship with her, gives us an insight into (spoiler alert) what went wrong with her relationship with Rumford:[9]

Il faut bien vous aimer d'amour, avec une nuance ou avec l'autre. J'ai l'experience que vous n'êtes pas proper a l'amitié. Vous n'avez ni épanchements, ni son intérêt, ni ses consolations, ni ses conseils, ni ses caresses, ni ses discours, ni son doux silence. Ou cesse votre tendresse, tout cesse. Vous devenez froide, dure, querelleuse, et c'est l'expression désobligeante qui arrive d'ell-même sur vos lèvres.

We have shown the original here to highlight du Pont's use of the formal "vous," which indicates the state of their relationship at this time. Our rough translation (though it reads better in French) is:

You have to love and be loved with passion, with one nuance or with the other. I have seen that you are not fit for friendship. You have none of its effusion, its interest, its consolations, nor its advice, its caresses, its speeches, nor its sweet silence. When your affection stops, everything stops. You become cold, hard, quarrelsome, and an unkind expression appears on your lips.

This was the character of the woman, now restored to a society that was itself consciously putting the events of the recent past behind it, that Rumford fell for a couple of years later. It is time for us to pick up the thread of our narrative once again from his perspective.

CHAPTER 9

Paris Match

RUMFORD RETURNED TO LONDON ON DECEMBER 20, 1801, INTENDING to stay only long enough to put his affairs in order before returning to Paris and Marie Lavoisier. Significantly, there is no evidence that he visited, or even corresponded with, Lady Palmerston during his time in England, during which he entirely focused on work. His relationship with Lady Palmerston may have cooled not least because of Rumford's tactless habit of singing the praises of the beautiful ladies of Paris in his letters to her.

The attention—or lack of attention—that his work received at this time can only have encouraged his plans to make Paris his new base. One of his priorities was to put his essays and other papers in order for publication, but he had fallen so far off the radar that his publishers, Cadell and Davies, said there was no demand for such a book, and only reluctantly agreed to publish his *Philosophical Papers*, a gathering together of his various papers for the Royal Society. He also finished his essays on domestic improvements, the benefits of warm baths, and other matters of only passing interest here. That includes his Essay XII,[1] in which he explains that building large fires in winter does "little more than increase the volume of those streams of cold air which come whistling in through every crevice of the doors and windows," and points out that if all these openings were sealed up a small fire could keep a large room comfortably warm. Advice that still had not been properly taken on board by house-builders in England in the 1950s.

Early 1802 saw the production of the most accurate drawing of Rumford, and the least accurate account of his life. He was more than willing to oblige a request from the artist by sitting for the drawing, and delighted that the result was intended for publication. One of Pictet's students, Augustin de Candolle, visited Rumford to obtain a biographical sketch to accompany the picture, and as de Candolle much later revealed, Rumford himself wrote the self-glorifying biography, then made the student copy it out in his own handwriting so that its origin would be concealed. The result was what Sanborn Brown describes as "the most fictitious biography of Rumford that has ever been written"; it is not worth discussing except for the insight the anecdote gives into Rumford's character.

It was the same thirst for recognition by posterity that saw him doing everything he could at this time to ensure that the reputation of the Royal Institution (RI) survived, even if the RI itself could not survive in the form he had hoped. By 1802 failure was a distinct possibility. The workshops were unfinished, money was a problem, and by now the prospect of a school for mechanics had become so remote that Webster was fired. For public consumption, Rumford put on a bold front, writing in the *Philosophical Magazine* in April 1802 that the RI may "be considered as finished and firmly established." In fact, at that time the RI had outstanding bills totaling £3,900 and a bank account containing only £3,180. It was clear that drastic changes to his original scheme were needed if the RI were to survive at all, and equally clear that he was not the man to carry through those changes. We shall look at those changes in the coda; for now, like Rumford in 1802, we shall focus on events in mainland Europe. After packing up in Brompton Row and making a detailed inventory of its contents, ready to send for anything he wanted later but keeping the house on so that he could visit London again, he left England on May 9, having been in London for less than five months, and, as it happened, never returned. He left the RI, as Bence Jones wrote in a letter to Ellis:

> *Without any workshops, or mechanics' institute, or kitchen, or model exhibition, but with experimental researches, libraries, and a*

mineralogical collection, which were, according to Rumford's ideas,
for the benefit of the rich, and by no means capable of doing good to
the poor,—the object he had in view in his society for the diffusion of
useful knowledge.

Rumford himself traveled light and fast to Paris, with his heavy baggage, in two carriages, and servants following behind. His plan was to meet up with Blagden and spend a short time in France before heading to Munich with his friend. But once again his presence in the French capital proved useful to the Bavarian elector. Napoleon now controlled much of Europe, and Maximilian, as a good friend of the French, was negotiating through his representative in Paris a land grab that would push out the Bavarian border near Lichtenstein. Rumford was roped into the negotiations, delaying his departure. In spite of his presence as a de facto Bavarian diplomat, at this time Rumford's British citizenship proved an embarrassment. Napoleon's ambitions were increasingly running into opposition organized from London, and although Rumford was received at court he was welcomed civilly, rather than enthusiastically, while his baggage from London and his mail were subject to harassing time-wasting inspection by customs officials. He found a solution by having all the items sent to him from the RI addressed for the Bavarian minister in Paris. At one level, it must have been a relief to set out with Blagden on their delayed trip on August 10, 1802. But that was not the whole story. In spite of all the inconveniences that had been put in his way in France, and the much more welcoming reception that he had received in Bavaria, he wrote to his daughter on November 30 that he "would rather be in Paris; and the *certain lady* would rather have him there."[2]

In Munich, although Rumford was indeed warmly welcomed, he now had no official position and no responsibilities. After a leisurely journey, he arrived with Blagden on August 23, and spent a month showing his friend the sights, including the thriving English Garden, before settling down to some serious scientific investigation—or natural philosophy, as his contemporaries would have called it.

In a letter to Joseph Banks dated August 30,[3] Blagden wrote:

It is really pleasant to see with what respect and affection Count Rumford is treated here by all ranks of people. I do not mean to say that he is without enemies, for surely he has many, but all, as far as I can learn, from envy, jealousy, or competition of interests. The great mass of people consider him as a public benefactor, and would rejoice to see the government of the country thrown into his hands.

But it was science, not politics, that Rumford engaged in. Always fascinated by heat, he now tried to find out if there was any difference between the heat provided by the bright sun and the invisible warmth of a stove. In the course of these experiments he prepared cylindrical wooden boxes that were half-filled with threads of silver obtained from old lace, separated from the empty bottom of the cylinder by thin sheets of either polished brass, polished tinned iron, or plain dull iron—he knew that these materials had different capacities to store heat, so that it takes longer to warm some than others, and that if they were all at the same temperature the iron, in this case, would hold more heat than the other two metals. Sensitive thermometers were mounted upright in the silver threads, and everything was insulated with fur except the exposed metal discs. When the boxes were laid on their sides, the warming rays of the sun or the heat from a stove could strike the metal surfaces. Rumford found that the thermometers behaved in the same way when the discs were exposed to either the warmth of the sun or the heat from a stove. But then serendipity struck.

One day in October, shortly after Blagden had left Munich, Rumford had warmed all three boxes to the same temperature in the sunlight, then put them in a corner of the room, standing upright, to cool down. A little later he happened to glance at them and "to my no slight astonishment, I saw the box which before contained the most heat (the one which had the iron disc) was now the coldest of all."[4] This led to a series of experiments that by early 1803 had confirmed that the shinier a surface is, the more slowly it loses heat. Ever practically minded, Rumford pointed out that steam radiators should be painted black to encourage them to give out heat, but the pipes carrying the steam should be shiny, to minimize heat loss en route. Similarly, he said, a shiny teapot will retain heat better than an equivalent dull teapot. This work later also led him into a mild eccentricity when he took to wearing white clothes in winter, including a shiny white hat, to keep himself warm.

During the rest of the winter, Rumford devoted a lot of time to inventing different kinds of thermometer, which had some practical uses at the time but did not provide any new insights into the physical world. He was essentially filling in time until the spring in order to meet the residence requirement for his Bavarian pension—his promise to spend six months each year in Bavaria. His letters show how eager he was to get back to Paris and Marie Lavoisier, but on May 16 war again broke out between Britain and France. This time, there were no concessions even for a retired Bavarian general, and Rumford was denied access to France. Worse, as Napoleon now controlled much of Europe, there was no way he could get to England by any reasonably direct route. But Marie was able to obtain permission to travel to Munich, where she arrived early in June 1803, with further permission for her and Rumford to travel to Switzerland. Even the presence of Marie, however, did not distract Rumford from making keen observations of the world around them when they were met by Pictet and visited the glacier above Chamonix before heading to Geneva, where they arrived in August.

On the glacier, Rumford was intrigued by a phenomenon that he promptly explained and wrote up as a paper for the *Philosophical Transactions*, published the following year.[5] He noticed "a pit perfectly cylindrical, about seven inches in diameter and more than four feet deep, quite full of water." When he probed the inside with a pole, he found

> *that its sides were polished and that its bottom was hemispherical and well defined. The pit was not quite perpendicular to the plane of the horizon but inclined a little toward the south as it descended, and in consequence of this inclination, its mouth, or opening at the surface of the ice, was not circular but elliptical.*

Their guide told him that such pits were common on the glacier in summer, but "that they are frozen up and disappear on the return of winter." Rumford quickly understood why the pits occurred, drawing on the experiments in the late 1790s that had shown that as water cools it reaches a maximum density at a temperature slightly above the freezing point, and on his studies of convection (see chapter 6).

What Rumford realized was that when a little puddle of water formed in a depression on the glacier in summer, the top of the puddle would be kept relatively warm—just above freezing—by the air above it, while the bottom of the puddle, in contact with the ice beneath, would be at the freezing (or melting) point of water. Because of the peculiar properties of water, the liquid at the top of the puddle would not only be warmer than the liquid underneath, but denser. So it would sink down to the bottom of the puddle, while the freezing cold water at the bottom would rise to the surface. The warm water at the bottom would melt some of the ice, making the hole a tiny bit deeper, and cool close to freezing point as it did so. This would make it lighter, so before it could freeze it would rise up to the surface. But while this was going on the cold water at the top would be warmed and sink downward, continuing the cycle. It is a perfect example of inverted convection, with the overall effect being like a drill pushing a hole deeper and deeper into the glacier—until summer ended and the whole thing froze again.

The visit to Switzerland was largely a holiday, and has the flavor of the modern idea of a "pre-moon." But although Rumford had left England, his scientific prestige had been enhanced without any effort on his part. First, in November 1802 he had received the initial Rumford Medal of the Royal Society, for "his various Discoveries respecting Light and Heat." For those not in the know about the behind-the-scenes she-nanigans to ensure he got the award (and probably even for many who did have a hint of what was going on), this carried considerable cachet. He had also been elected as an associate member of the Royal Society of Göttingen and as a member of the Royal Society of Copenhagen. But best of all, for the future plans of Rumford and Marie Lavoisier, in January 1803, as part of a reorganization of the French Institute, he was made an associate member of the first class, which covered the mathematical and physical sciences. Napoleon, as we have seen, was something of a scientific groupie, and a member of the first class himself (on much the same basis that Rumford was the first recipient of the Rumford Medal).

All this convinced the couple that it would now be possible for Rumford to obtain permission to enter France. Marie went to Paris to lobby on his behalf, while Rumford waited in Mannheim, near the French border, for the anticipated approval. It came in November 1803, not until after Rumford had been invited to dine with the king and queen of Sweden, who were also in Mannheim.[6] Promising to keep out of politics and apply himself to natural philosophy, he was allowed to settle in Paris, with the immediate intention of marrying Marie. But bureaucratic delays put that ambition on hold while he concentrated on scientific work in the months that followed.

There was nothing particularly new or dramatic about any of this work, but Rumford seems to have been eager to establish himself as an active member of the first class of the institute, and presented several papers to them describing work he had done before—or variations on things he had done before—concerning heat, light, and sound. Under the revolutionary calendar in use at that time, seven-day weeks had been replaced by ten-day "decades," and the institute met twice every decade; between the beginning of March 1804 and the end of June that year Rumford made presentations on at least six occasions. Science, however, was far from being his only preoccupation in those months. Blagden wrote to Rumford's daughter on March 12[7] that he had received an account of her father that said he was "very assiduous in his attentions to the French lady, with whom, indeed, he spends most of his time," and that "he is entirely losing his interest in this country [England]."

Rumford and Marie had initially planned to get married in May, and he wrote to Sally[8] singing the praises of his prospective bride, describing her as

> *a widow, without children, never having had any; is about my own age, enjoys good health, is very pleasant in society, has a handsome fortune at her own disposal, enjoys a most respectable reputation, keeps a good house, which is frequented by all the first Philosophers and men of eminence in the science and literature of the age, is goodness itself. . . . [I]n short, she is another Lady Palmerston.*

Almost as an afterthought, he added, "[S]he is not bad-looking"; for once, it was the mind of a woman that had first attracted Rumford. But he also told Sally in another letter that "she appears to be most sincerely attached to me, and I esteem and love her very much."[9]

The "good house" is a reference to Marie Lavoisier's "salon." The salons of the period following the revolution were cultural hubs, often hosted by women, where the great and the good met, exchanging intellectual ideas and holding up the standards of good manners in polite society. Rumford greatly enjoyed such company when he chose to attend, quite apart from the attraction of Marie herself; but it would be a different matter when the gatherings were being held in his own house, whether he felt in the mood for them or not.

The wedding plans, however, soon ran into complications. The French authorities insisted that before the ceremony could go ahead Rumford had to supply copies of his own birth certificate and the death certificate of his first wife. All these records were on the other side of the Atlantic, and he had to write to Sally with an urgent request that she get hold of them and send them to him in Paris. He also needed the consent of his mother and the death certificate of his father, because the new French Civil Code insisted on parental permission. All this was spelled out, including the form of words to be used in the various certificates, in a letter Rumford sent to Sally on July 2. With British ships blockading France, communications between France and America were reduced to a trickle; it took nearly six months for the documents to arrive.

While the wedding was on hold, the political situation was far from static. Napoleon had reached the stage of power corrupting his behavior, and had proclaimed an empire (abolishing the republic) on May 18, 1804; he would crown himself (literally, in a lavishly over-the-top ceremony) as emperor on December 2 that year. Meanwhile, King Francis II of Austria had also proclaimed himself as an emperor, and there were political maneuverings for Austria, Russia, and Britain to join forces in a coalition against France (or, more specifically, against Napoleon). Bavaria, now technically neutral but essentially in the French sphere of influence and bordering on Austria, was in a decidedly awkward situation. But so was Rumford—as Brown has put it, he was "a retired English officer engaged to a famous French widow, living on a Bavarian army pension, and trying with all his energy to be friendly with Napoleon but holding the rank of count of the Holy Roman Empire, of which Francis of Austria was emperor." Unfortunately, we have no information about how Rumford himself felt about this state of affairs, because very little of his correspondence from the second half of 1804 survives, and he was less active in the institute. The contact with Sally was limited to getting the documents he needed, and there was no longer any communication with Lady Palmerston, who died, probably of cancer, in January 1805. One thing we do know is that his reputation in England suffered, unsurprisingly, from his French connection. In the March 12 letter mentioned earlier, Blagden had also commented to Sally,

His residence in Paris this winter, whilst we are threatened with an invasion, is considered by everyone as very improper conduct, and his numerous enemies do not fail to make the most of it. He has quarrelled with Mr. Bernard and others of his old friends at the Royal Institution, and they do all they can to render him unpopular.

Rumford's situation was made even more complicated because by early 1805 he was due to make his annual visit to Munich, required by the terms of his pension. He delayed as long as possible in the hope of getting married first and taking Marie with him, providing some insurance against the possibility of being denied entry back into France. But the elector Maximilian, in spite of all the other things he had to worry about (or perhaps because this was one thing he could control), insisted, and in June 1805 Rumford returned to Bavaria, still unmarried and without Marie. Once again, he had no official duties and spent his time writing scientific articles and carrying out one particularly neat experiment, clearly inspired by his observations on the Chamonix glacier, which provided an accurate measurement of the temperature at which water reaches its maximum density.

Rumford filled a container with ice on the point of melting, exactly at the freezing point of water. Inside the ice bath there was a second container, full of ice-cold water, and inside that was a little cup-shaped receptacle, in contact with a thermometer. Directly above the cup there was a heated ball that could be dipped into the liquid at the top of the inner vessel and warm the water there. As Rumford anticipated the warm water was denser than the icy water and flowed down into the cup; the densest water filled the cup, where its temperature could be measured. He found that the cup filled with water at 41 degrees Fahrenheit, equivalent to about 5 degrees Celsius (modern measurements give the temperature at which water has its maximum density as just under 4 degrees Celsius, so he did remarkably well with the equipment he had available).[10] His paper reporting this work was read to the institute in Paris in July. It wouldn't be long before he was back there himself.

Meanwhile, while Rumford was away Marie had been tidying up some loose ends from Antoine Lavoisier's life. The timing may have been a coincidence, but it neatly draws a line under one relationship just at the time a new relationship was about to be formalized. At the time of his arrest, Antoine, with Marie's help, had been preparing his "Mémoires," a considerably revised and updated collection of his chemical works, for publication. At the beginning of the nineteenth century, with Antoine formally rehabilitated and recognized as a great scientist, Marie was determined to complete as much of this project as she could, and put together two volumes from the material Antoine had prepared. Unfortunately, she included a preface containing a stinging condemnation of half a dozen chemists who she felt had contributed to Antoine's fate by their failure to speak up on his behalf; this was so scathing that no commercial publisher would touch the book at a time when, as Rumford had noticed, the revolution was regarded by polite society as best forgotten. Marie had the book printed in two volumes at her own expense anyway, and, starting in 1803, donated copies to the libraries of many institutions and to individual scientists. These included the members of the institute, the École Polytechnique and the Bibliothéque Impériale in Paris, one to Charles Blagden, and twenty-four copies for Rumford's friend Pictet. In 1805, she was persuaded to remove the offending preface, and the book was published commercially as *Mémoires de physique et de chimie*. It was Antoine's last word on chemistry, appearing in the same year that Marie would formally start a new life with another great scientist.

By then, things were coming to a head in Bavaria. In September Francis II gave up any hope of persuading Maximilian to come in to the anti-French coalition, and sent his troops into Bavaria. The elector and his court fled to Mannheim, but Rumford was one jump ahead. He wrote to Sally, "Foreseeing the Storm, I left Munich the day before the Elector left it. I have brought Aichner [his longtime servant] and his whole family. . . . I succeeded in so winding up my affairs in Bavaria as in the future to be able to live where I please."[11] The requirement to spend part of each year in Munich had been rescinded. Even better, when he got back to Paris in the middle of September he found that all the paperwork was in order so that the long anticipated marriage could take place. He was fifty-two, she was forty-seven, and they were joined in a quiet ceremony, but a notable event in Parisian society, on October 24, 1805.[12] London society was less than impressed. Announcing the event, the *Literary Tablet* commented:

> *Married; in Paris, Count Rumford to the widow of Lavoisier; by which nuptial experiment he obtains a fortune of 8,000 pounds per annum—the most effective of all the Rumfordizing projects for keeping a house warm.*

Apart from the sour grapes on the other side of the Channel, everything seemed set fair for the couple to live happily ever after—but it was not to be.

Endgame

WITH HINDSIGHT, WE CAN SEE A HINT OF WHAT WAS TO COME WHEN Marie insisted that after her marriage she would be known as Marie Lavoisier de Rumford, retaining her first husband's name along with her formal new title as Countess de Rumford. As the Count of Amerval had discovered all those years earlier, Marie usually got her own way. But Rumford, too, was used to getting his own way. The irresistible force was about to meet the immovable object, with predictable results.

With Marie's fortune divided equally between them, and Rumford's income enhanced by an increase in his pension by 4,000 florins as a wedding present from Maximilian, the couple set up home in a large house with extensive gardens.[1] The day after the wedding, in a letter to Sally, Rumford described his new home as[2]

> *all but a paradise. Removed from the noise and bustle of the street, facing full to the South, in the midst of a beautiful garden of more than two acres, well planted with trees and shrubbery. The entrance from the street is through an iron gate, by a beautiful winding avenue, well planted, and the porter's lodge is by the side of this gate; a great bell to be rung in case of ceremonious visits.*

But trouble began almost immediately. Rumford enthusiastically set about remodeling the house and kitchens in line with his own ideas, writing to Sally in December:

The house is rather an old-fashioned concern, built in a plot of two acres of land, in the very centre of the very finest part of Paris, near the Champs Elysées and the Tuileries and principal boulevards. I have already made great alterations in our place, and shall do a vast deal more. When these are done, I think Madame de Rumford will find it in a very different condition from that in which it was.

Unfortunately, in her eyes "different" was not necessarily better, and the building work interfered with her established routine as the hostess of a fashionable salon. Every Monday, she gave a formal dinner for up to a dozen luminaries, including foreign visitors;[3] on Tuesday she was "at home" for anyone of the right sort who wished to call on her; and on Friday she had music—recitals played by the finest musicians for a large and appreciative audience. Rumford had no objection to attending such events from time to time, especially if it gave him an opportunity to elaborate on his own achievements, but having them so often, and being expected to be a considerate host, got under his skin. Rumford's favorite topic of conversation was Rumford and his achievements, and Marie is quoted as saying, "My Rumford would make me very happy could he but keep quiet."[4] His laboratory provided an escape from all these activities, but unlike Lavoisier he did not involve his wife in his work, which only added to the tension between them. She was not one to stay in the background, and was forthright in presenting her views, at home as well as in the world at large, where she still regarded herself as the keeper of the Lavoisier flame. As early as January 1806 Rumford wrote to his daughter:

Between you and myself, as a family secret, I am not at all sure that two certain persons were not wholly mistaken, in their marriage, as to each other's characters. Time will show. But two months barely expired, I forbode difficulties. Already I am obliged to send my good Germans home,—a great discomfort to me and wrong to them.

The "good Germans" were the Aichner family, whom Rumford had brought with him not only for his own comfort but to get them away from Munich when the Austrians invaded. But it was asking rather a lot to expect them to be integrated with the French servants in Marie's household, and in any case the situation in Bavaria had shifted against the Austrians. On December 10, 1805, Napoleon defeated the combined armies of Austria and Russia at Austerlitz, and Francis II had been obliged to give up any claims to Bavaria. The Aichners would be in no danger if they returned home, and although Rumford regarded them almost as family, home they went—except for one girl who stayed in the Rumfords' household and would be looked after by Marie even after the couple separated. The girl, Mary Sarah, was trained as a milliner and given a dowry of 20,000 francs by Marie when she married a young merchant.

Rumford retreated into his work, designing an improved oil lamp and lighting system that he described to the institute, and carrying out experiments involving surface tension and capillary action that led him (we now know) to incorrect conclusions. This resulted in a public disagreement with Pierre-Simon de Laplace, who turned out to be right. The debate highlighted the extent to which Rumford's old-fashioned way of investigation was being superseded by the more analytical, mathematical approach of the younger generation; he was, after all, now in his fifties, and would not make any further significant contribution to science, although he did continue to come up with practical suggestions for improving everyday life.

We don't know a great deal about Rumford's life over the next few years, because he was to some extent cold-shouldered by the French scientific establishment as a British scientist who had argued with Laplace and was also a main opponent of the idea of caloric, which Lavoisier had named and which still held sway in those quarters. Marie, loyal to Lavoisier's memory, continued to promote the idea in the teeth of Rumford's evidence, which added to the friction between them and also suggests that she was not as good a scientist as some wishful thinkers have suggested—certainly not Antoine's equal partner.

Rumford's correspondence with England was limited, although not entirely cut off by the war, and the blockade also made communication with America difficult. But none of this prevented a letter he wrote on

October 24, 1806, the first anniversary of his marriage to Marie, from reaching Sally:

> *This being the first year's anniversary of my marriage, from what I wrote two months after it you will be curious to know how things stand at present. I am sorry to say that experience only serves to confirm me in the belief that in character and natural propensities Madame de Rumford and myself are totally unlike, and never ought to have thought of marrying. We are, besides, both too independent, both in our sentiments and habits of life, to live peaceably together,— she having been mistress all her days of her actions and I, with no less liberty, leading for the most part the life of a bachelor. Very likely she is as much disaffected towards me as I am towards her. Little it matters with me, but I call her a female Dragon,—simply by that gentle name! We have got to the pitch of my insisting on one thing and she on another.*
>
> *It is possible that, had the war ceased raging, and had we gone to Italy, where she is dying to go, and with me too, she having heard me speak much of the delights of that country,—she having been very happy, too, in travelling with me in Switzerland,—it might have suspended difficulties, but never have effected a cure. That is out of the question. Indeed, I have not the least idea of continuing here, and, if possible, still less the wish, and am only planning in my mind what step I shall take next,—to be hoped more to my advantage. Communication with England is prohibited, and it makes me sad.*

About this time, Rumford also made an intriguing observation that he didn't follow up but that provides a link to the modern understanding of heat as a form of motion. In a series of experiments, reported to the institute in March 1807, he suspended small flakes of wax in a mixture of water and alcohol so that they floated without falling or rising. He noticed that the flakes moved about very slowly in a random pattern, and thought that he had discovered perpetual motion. What he had actually observed was a phenomenon now known as Brownian motion, which almost a century later Albert Einstein explained as being caused by suspended pieces of dust or other material being buffeted unevenly by the molecules of the liquid in which they floated. This was clinching evidence, in the first decade of the twentieth century, of the reality of atoms and molecules. And the hotter the fluid is the faster the molecules move. Without knowing it, Rumford had found evidence in support of his theory of heat, as well as evidence for the reality of atoms. He did later follow up this observation with experiments in which he demonstrated that when a layer of fresh water is floated on top of a layer of denser salt water the two liquids eventually mix, which left him perplexed but is also a result of the random movement of the molecules. But that was as far as he went. His next presentation to the institute was a demonstration that gilded porcelain containers cool more slowly in air than plain dull pots, but that if both vessels were plunged into water they cooled at the same rate, demonstrating a difference between cooling by radiation and cooling by conduction, which he argued could not be explained in terms of a loss of "caloric." If this was not enough to alienate his audience, his next appearance as a speaker at the institute literally made him a laughingstock.

During his experiments with lighting, Rumford had used frosted glass covers—lampshades—for various oil lamps, to diffuse the light they provided and make it less harsh. He had found that this let just as much light through as plain glass, and realized that in some circumstances they could provide more light. He used the example of a room that only had windows looking onto a small courtyard with no direct sunlight, where panes of "roughened" glass would diffuse more light into the room than panes of plain glass. On August 14, 1807, Rumford gave a talk at the institute outlining a series of ideas to improve the heating and lighting of the lecture room, along the lines of the improvements he had overseen at the RI. When he got to the lighting, he said:

> *Since the hall is surrounded by very high buildings which are close to it, there is a deficiency of light in the hall which is very noticeable. . . . [By] using panes of ground glass for the outside windows, the amount of light in the hall would be much increased, and the light will be more equable, softer, and more agreeable.*

His words were greeted with laughter. He was, of course, correct, but "common sense" told the learned academicians that he was wrong. He didn't make another presentation to them for three and a half years.

On October 24, 1807, Rumford wrote another "wedding anniversary" letter to his daughter, highlighting how far his relationship with Marie had deteriorated:

> *I am still here, and so far from things getting better they become worse every day. We are more violent and more open, and more public, as may really be said, in our quarrels. If she does not mind publicity, for a certainty I shall not. As I write the uncouth word quarrels, I will give you an idea of one of them.*
>
> *In the first place, be it known that this estate is a joint concern. I have as good a right to it as Madame,—she having paid rather more in the beginning, but I an immensity of money in repairs and alterations, &c., &c., besides a great deal of my own time and care spent while we have been here.*
>
> *I am almost afraid to tell you the story, my good child, lest in future you should not be good; lest what I am about relating should set you a bad example, make you passionate, and so on. But I had been made very angry. A large party had been invited I neither liked nor approved of, and invited for the sole purpose of vexing me. Our house being in the centre of the garden, walled around, with iron gates, I put on my hat, walked down to the porter's lodge and gave him orders, on his peril, not to let anyone in. Besides, I took away the keys. Madame went down, and when the company arrived she talked with them,— she on one side, they on the other, of the high brick wall. After that she goes and pours boiling water on some of my beautiful flowers.*

By this time, it seems that Rumford was already trying to work out the details of a legal separation that would secure his share of their combined resources. Although living in the same house, Rumford and Marie now increasingly led separate lives, and he dined alone, unless Mary Sarah joined him. But on a happier note, throughout all these difficulties he had been able to maintain some contact with London, and learned about his protégé Davy's pioneering work with electrolysis.[5] In January 1808 he wrote to Pictet, "The beautiful discovery of Davy has caused a great sensation here. I have assisted in one of the experiments performed at the École Polytechnique by Gay-Lussac and Thénard" (involving the extraction of potassium from its salt). Davy, as we mentioned earlier, had been using a powerful battery based on Rumford's design.

This provided a rare lighter note in gloomy times. A few weeks later, he wrote to Sally,

It is impossible to continue in this way, and we shall separate. I only wish it was well over. It is probable I shall take a house at Auteuil, a very pleasant place, with the Seine on one side and the Bois de Boulogne on the other, about a league[6] from Paris. I have seen a very handsome house there which I can have—rather dear, but that matters little can I but find quiet.

The house, 59 Rue d'Auteuil, had an interesting history. A previous resident had been Anne-Catherine Helvétius, a widow who was the mistress of Benjamin Franklin when he lived in Paris—Franklin himself stayed at another house in Auteuil from 1777 to 1785. Number 59 was the house where, according to a famous anecdote, Madame Helvétius asked Franklin why he wouldn't stay the night, to which he replied that he was waiting until the nights were longer. The quip was almost worthy of Molière—who, as it happens, had also lived in Auteuil. The village, as it then was, was a fashionable location.

Rumford duly took over the lease on a wing of the house and gardens at the end of April 1808, but he did not actually move in until the following year. Ellis tells us that Rumford was seriously ill for several months in 1808, although we do not have details of what was wrong, and spent the winter of 1808–1809 convalescing before he moved out of the matrimonial home. It was during this winter that he refined his designs for coffee makers, making full use of his understanding of heat and convection, as well as his own love of coffee, to produce a range of designs from large pots based on the drip principle and holding several cups to a portable single-cup coffee maker with its own alcohol-fueled burner.

During the spring of 1809, as Rumford wrote to Sally, he was at the house in Auteuil "most every day from morning till night," but it was only on June 30 that he formally separated from his wife[7] and officially started to spend the night there, "relieved from an almost insupportable burden." He continued:

I cannot repeat how happy I am,—gaining every day in health, which from vexations had been seriously deranged. I am persuaded it is all for the best. After the scenes which I have recently passed through, I realise, as never before, the sweets of quiet, liberty, and independence. My household consists of the most faithful, honest people, attached to me, without dissension, bribery, or malice. And, above all, [without] that eternal contradiction. Oh! happy, thrice happy, am I, to be my own man again!

The terms of the separation meant that Rumford kept his share of the money, but gave up his interest in the house he had shared with Marie. He now had several hundred thousand francs invested in the French funds (accounts vary as to his total wealth), and in this independent and happy state, he urged his daughter to come and join him. In her own memoir, she says, "He invites me to come to him if I can consent to be his companion in perfect solitude, even obscurity. Otherwise I was not to come." But this caution did not deter her, although she did not leave America until the summer of 1811.

With his personal life seemingly settled, Rumford still had to sort out his financial affairs and other obligations. Since his marriage, the political map of Europe had been redrawn. After Austerlitz, Bavaria had not only gained territory and (seemingly) security, but a king, as Napoleon elevated Maximilian to that status on January 1, 1806. This was part of a widespread reorganization in which Napoleon created the Confederation of the Rhine, a group of sixteen German states friendly to France, plucked from the Holy Roman Empire, which, Napoleon proclaimed in July that year, no longer existed. On August 6 Francis II accepted the inevitable and abdicated, to become Francis I of Austria. From that date, Rumford was count of an empire that did not exist.

This naturally led him to worry that his pension from Bavaria might also cease to exist, and, of course, there had been no way for him to receive his half-pay from England since hostilities between Britain and France had recommenced in 1803. In his capacity as king, Maximilian had visited Paris and taken the trouble to reassure Rumford that his status in Bavaria was unchanged, but now that Rumford's domestic problems were resolved he wanted to secure his position there, and took the opportunity to visit Munich in August 1810. His principle motive seems to have been to establish a relationship with the crown prince, Ludwig, who was then twenty-four and who would become Ludwig I (the second king of Bavaria) in 1825. Rumford had already been in correspondence with the prince, offering him unsolicited advice on how to handle the problem of the Bavarian poor.

He found that much had changed in Munich, and wrote to Sally that Countess Nogarola had died; that his daughter Sophy, now twenty-one, was married, but ill; that his reception had been "most kind and flattering"; and that

> everybody here of your old acquaintance enquires after you. The three aides-de-camp I had when you were with me, Taxis, Spreti, and Verger, have all been killed in the late wars. The Bavarian troops, who have distinguished themselves by their bravery on all occasions, have suffered greatly.[8] Munich grows larger every day. The English Garden is in the highest beauty.
>
> My health is perfectly good, and I am very happy. All my late sufferings are forgotten. I feel just as if relieved from an insupportable weight. God be thanked for my delivery!

On October 2 he also wrote to Pictet, who was living and working in Paris at that time, with what was by Rumford's standards a remarkable admission that he may have been in the wrong in his dealings with the institute, where Pictet was trying to mend bridges for him:[9]

> The misfortune I have had in France [his marriage] has so cruelly upset my spirit and courage that one should not be astonished at

my having expressed several times too publicly, my feelings and my indignation at the injustice I have been done.... Upon my return to Paris, I shall present myself to my colleagues, and shall take part in their discussions, hoping that one will always find me an eager lover of science and a cultured man, fit to live in society.

The explanation for this distinct mellowing in Rumford's character may be provided by another short letter he wrote from Munich to Paris, beginning with greetings to "my good Victoire" and ending, "Adieu, my good Victoire, take care of everything I pray you. Write to me from time to time to let me know how everything is going at home."[10] The recipient of the letter has sometimes been described as Rumford's housekeeper in Auteuil, but in the sense that she was in charge of "the most faithful, honest people" that made up his household, not that she did the dusting. Officially, she lived in the porter's lodge. Among other things, she filled the house with flowers and had caged birds singing for Rumford's enjoyment. Victoire's surname is variously spelled Lefèvre, Lefebvre, or Lefebre, but she is only rarely referred to and remains a shadowy figure in Rumford's life, even though she eventually bore his only son. The bottom line is that she undoubtedly made his remaining years happy ones.

Rumford left Munich at the end of October 1810, and returned to Paris via Turin, Nice, Toulon, Marseilles, Montpelier, Avignon, and Lyon. Now fifty-seven, he was back to his old self, if a little mellower, in good health, eager to join in the scientific activities and debates of the institute, and even back on friendly terms with Laplace. On April 15, 1811, more than four years after his previous presentation to them, he described to the institute the fruits of studies he had carried out on his recent travels concerning the efficiency of different kinds of wheels. Still unable to take a "holiday" without experimenting along the way, Rumford had invented an original dynamometer that measured the effort being put in by his horses to pull his carriage. At the time, there was a debate about whether wide wheels or narrow ones were more efficient, and there was also a problem with narrow wheels making ruts in the road surface. Wider wheels would obviously alleviate that problem, but there was a widespread belief that they would cause more friction, as well as being heavier, so they would make it harder for horses to pull their loads. Rumford carried out tests with three sets of wheels, one with rims an inch wide, one twice as wide, and one with four-inch rims. His experiments showed that wide rims were best and made it easier for the horses to pull carriages and wagons; but he was well aware that there was a general opinion that narrow wheels looked better. In spite of his efforts, this aesthetic objection prevented his idea catching on, although he put it into practice himself. Together with his white winter clothing, his habit of traveling around Paris in an unfashionable wide-wheeled carriage enhanced a reputation for eccentricity in the last years of his life.

We know a little more about those last years because Sally arrived from America on December 1, 1811, and kept a journal, as well as wrote letters home, which have survived. Her journey had not been easy. She traveled first to Philadelphia, in the early summer of 1811, then joined the *Drummond*, which sailed from New York on July 24. The ship was captured by the British brig *Cadmus* off Bordeaux on August 24, and taken into Plymouth on September 5 as a blockade runner.[11] Although treated courteously (she was, after all, a countess in her own right, and a neutral), Sally had her jewels and other property confiscated. Seemingly unfazed by any of this, she visited London, checked up on the house in Brompton Row, and went to the theater. Blagden, who had been ill, was recuperating at the house of a friend in Maidenhead, but wrote to her with advice, and introduced her to another friend, Admiral Sir Charles Pole, who helped her with the formalities that had to be completed before she could recover her possessions and continue to France. A week after she arrived in Auteuil, she wrote a letter to James Baldwin, Loammi's son, that gives details of the adventure. She "found friends everywhere, and not half so many difficulties as I was led to expect from the difficulty of the times"; refers to "a charming visit in London"; and says that the only tedious part of the journey was waiting in Plymouth for a fair wind, not being able to leave until November 12. Apart from that "all my journeys were prosperous and pleasant. I think I never had so pleasant a one in my life as from Plymouth to London. . . . I have really been in a number of fine cities since I saw you,—Philadelphia, New York, London, and now

Paris. It is quite amusing to me to be able to compare all the places one with another."

The news Sally brought from America was less amusing. Loammi Baldwin had died, and Rumford's mother, although healthy, was in need of money. This prompted Rumford to write to James Baldwin, who was a merchant in Boston, asking him to act as go-between and sending him a power of attorney so that he could establish a trust fund for Rumford's mother, with a capital of $10,000 and interest paid to her. This gives some idea of Rumford's own wealth at this time. In February 1812, though, Rumford changed his mind and transferred the whole of the stock to his mother with no strings attached. Ellis quotes from the letter Rumford sent to his mother at that time:

> *I desire that you will accept of it as a token of my dutiful affection for you, and of my gratitude for the kind care you took of me in the early part of my life. I have the greatest satisfaction in being able to show my gratitude for all your goodness to me, and to contribute to your ease and comfort. I request that you will consider this donation as being perfectly free and unconditional, and that you would enjoy and dispose of what is now your property just as you shall think best.*

It is signed "your dutiful and affectionate child, Benjamin." The gift came just in time. Rumford's mother died the following year, and the "property" passed to his Pierce half-siblings, which can only have encouraged them to think well of their brother.

Apart from personal news, Sally brought letters from several of Rumford's American friends and fellow scientists. These included Robert Livingston, a politician who had been the US ambassador to France between 1801 and 1804, but whose other interests included financing the inventor Robert Fulton to build early steamboats. Fulton's *North River Steamboat* is now regarded as the first successful commercial vessel of its kind; in 1807 it carried passengers from New York City to Albany on the Hudson River, and back again, a round trip of 300 miles (480 kilometers), in sixty-two hours. Rumford wrote back to congratulate Livingston on the success of this venture, and to describe his own success with wide-wheeled carriages. Sally was less than impressed by the carriage, and seems to have been embarrassed to be seen in it. She was also embarrassed by the presence in the household of Victoire Lefèvre, whom she describes as a "young person—either housekeeper, companion, or both." Sally was thirty-seven when she arrived in Paris in 1811, but we can only guess what age Victoire was to qualify as a "young person" in her eyes. Much later, after her father died, Sally got to know Victoire better; a young woman who lived in Sally's household at that time[12] wrote a partially fictionalized account describing how at the age of twenty-two Victoire had left Normandy, in the company of her younger sister and a friend, and made her way to Paris; but the anecdote does not say how she came to be in Rumford's household. As she was there, and provided all the companionship Rumford seemed to require, Sally found herself often at a loose end, and took long trips around Europe.

Sally's assessment of Marie is warmer than might have been expected:

> *I had not been many days at Auteuil before we had a visit from his separated lady, for they seemed to be on good terms, at least, on visiting terms. The lady was gracious to me, and I was charmed with her, nor did I ever find reason to be otherwise, for she was a truly remarkable character. Their disagreements must have arisen from their independence of character and means, being used always to having their own ways. Their pursuits in some particulars were different. He was fond of his experiments, and she of company. . . .*
>
> *It was a fine match, could they but have agreed. It was said by everybody, both friends and foes, that though the first flush of youth was past, it was decidedly a love-match.*

Rumford himself now seldom left Auteuil except to attend the regular meetings of the institute. He received only a few visitors—including Lagrange, and the same Thomas Underwood who had recommended Davy to the RI, who was also stranded in Paris by the war—but continued to contribute papers, mostly on minor topics and often repeating with slight variations themes he had published before. Many of these contributions were published privately in a series of papers, but only a few had any real impact on science. One of these described his invention of a device to measure accurately the amount of heat given off by a certain quantity of material when it burned—a calorimeter. But his most significant work at this time involved lamps and lighting, developing the ideas that he had presented to the Royal Society in the 1790s. In 1811 he also spelled out in more detail his definition of a "standard candle" (see page 83), first in a talk to the institute on October 14 (which was not published), then in a paper read at the Royal Society in January 1812,[13] and duly published by them. In this presentation, Rumford showed, among other things, that the amount of light given off by a lamp is affected by the temperature of the flame—a hotter flame gives more light:

The greatest light may be obtained by preserving the heat of the flame. Thus several flat flames placed together, in order that they may mutually cover and defend each other against the powerful cooling influences of surrounding bodies, form a lamp that has answered far beyond my most sanguine expectations.

I lose no time in giving an account of the principles on which it is constructed, in hopes that others may be induced to assist in improving it.

So far from being jealous of their success I shall rejoice in it, and shall ever be most ready to contribute to it by all the means in my power.

Because he already knew that flames were transparent, and did not block out the light from another flame, Rumford had constructed oil lamps with several wicks side by side, which burned very hot and bright; with air circulating up between each pair of wicks, the lamps were also very clean and produced no smoke or smell. He reported that one of his "polyflame" lamps (Rumford preferred the term "illuminators") gave more light "than that of 52 wax candles, and this without the least appearance of either smoke or smell."

Rumford saw this as a potential boon to humankind, and was eager, as with all his inventions, that it should be freely available for anyone who needed it. He had no time for patents, either for himself or anyone else, and was interested in the common good. This explains how the work came to be published by the Royal Society when Britain and France were still at war. On November 1, 1811, Rumford demonstrated his polyflame lamps to Jonathan Russell, the US ambassador in Paris, who was about to depart for London.[14] He gave Russell a sealed package containing his paper, with instructions that the seal should only be broken at the RI just before the meeting where it was to be read. This put the invention in the public domain, making it impossible for anyone to patent the idea and profit by it.

Rumford had every reason to take these precautions, as a dispute about the rights to an earlier kind of lamp that he had invented was brewing up in 1811. The details of the design are not important now, but the crucial point is that Rumford's design was described in a paper presented to the institute on March 24, 1806. Another inventor, Isaac Bordier-Marcet (usually known as Bordier), working entirely independently and knowing nothing of Rumford's work, came up with a very similar idea that he demonstrated at an exposition in Paris on May 25, 1806. Bordier won a prize for his invention, and although the similarity with Rumford's design was soon recognized, both variations on the theme went into production, Bordier in collaboration with a man called Pallebot while Rumford's version was made by Jerome Parquet. Rumford was happy, as usual, to see the idea freely available to all. But in 1809 Bordier was issued with a patent for the design, which would have entitled him to royalties on sales of Rumford's version. In 1812 a group of ten lamp manufacturers, headed by Parquet, sued Bordier and Pallebot on the grounds that the patent was invalid because Rumford had described the key features of the lamps first. A flavor of the proceedings can be gleaned from the defense attorney's attempt to have the case dismissed because, he claimed, Rumford had criminally incited people to break the law:

> *M. de Rumford, who does not believe in patents, and who regards most people as pirates made rich at his expense, concludes his work with the following reflection "I desire only that the whole world should profit by it, without preventing others from using it with equal freedom." . . . A foreigner, whom France has heaped with*

honours, dares to invite the artisans of France to violate the laws of the land! . . . You may (he tells them in so many words) manufacture the objects described in Bordier's patent. . . .[15]

Playing the patriotic card is often the desperate resort of someone with a weak argument, and so it proved on this occasion. Rumford's side won the case, and thanks to his precautions no similar problems would arise with the polyflame illuminator.

During 1812, while Napoleon was engaged on his disastrous Russian adventure, Rumford continued to experiment with heat, burning all kinds of fuel to measure their effectiveness. Ether proved too effective—it caused an explosion that sent flames shooting to the ceiling and almost set the house on fire. There was nothing of any great scientific significance in any of this work, but it led to what turned out to be Rumford's last presentation to the institute, on November 30, 1812—eight days before Napoleon abandoned the remnants of his army and set off back to Paris. Rumford's interests were now largely domestic. He pulled together all his designs for coffee makers in a paper titled "Excellent Qualities of Coffee and the Act of Making It in the Highest Perfection," which was eventually published as his Essay XVIII;[16] spent a lot of time in his garden, where he was particularly proud of his roses; and as the months of 1813 passed paid particular attention to Victoire, who was now pregnant. This concrete evidence of the relationship between her father, now sixty, and Victoire made Sally so uncomfortable that as soon as the pregnancy began to show she left on an extended visit to Switzerland, and stayed away for more than a year. The baby, a boy whose name was given on the birth certificate as Charles François Robert Lefebvre, was born on October 13, 1813, a few days before the thirty-ninth birthday of his half-sister, Sally. The father's name was not given on the certificate. This was also a few days before Napoleon's decisive defeat by coalition forces at the Battle of Leipzig, which raged from October 16 to 19.

Even though Napoleon's empire was crumbling as the war continued, life in Paris (at least for people like Rumford) was largely unaffected, and before the Battle of Leipzig had turned the tide Napoleon had given permission for Humphry Davy, as an eminent scientist, to visit France and Italy to study volcanic structures. Accompanied by his wife and by his assistant Michael Faraday, Davy set out from London on the day Charles Lefèvre was born, and arrived in Paris on October 27, delayed en route by officials who at first could not believe that the passport issued by Napoleon was genuine. On November 10, Davy and Faraday, accompanied by Underwood, took dinner with Rumford, and were shown around his laboratory. This is the last incident in Rumford's life that we have a direct record of.[17] As it finally dawned on Paris society that the war was about to come to them, Sally had gone to the safety of Le Havre, and Marie had also left the city. On March 31, 1814, the Russian army entered Paris (with less fighting than its residents had feared) and Napoleon abdicated on April 6. In the confusion that followed, and with Sally and Marie away, we have no record of Rumford's activities until the news that he died of a fever on August 21, 1814. He was buried in the local cemetery three days later, with Sally and Marie still away. In London, the September issue of the *Monthly Magazine, or British Register* carried the following notice:

> *At his seat in Paris, 60 [he was actually 61], died, August 21, that illustrious philosopher, Benjamin Thompson, Count Rumford, F. R. S., Member of the Institute, &c., an American by birth, but the friend of man, and an honour to the whole human race.*

EPILOGUE

Generations

WHAT HAPPENED TO RUMFORD'S CHILDREN AND THEIR DESCENDANTS? We know a little bit about them from Sally's memoir, and a bit less from official records, but the trail goes cold early in the twentieth century. We also have to be cautious about taking everything Sally writes at face value because she had a tendency to romanticize. But there is another, more factual, account, provided by someone who was in effect (though not legally) Sally Rumford's adopted daughter. Her married name was Emma Burgum, and her writings are held in the archives of the New Hampshire Historical Society; their highlights have been summarized by Merrill.

The story begins just after Rumford's death, when Sally decided to fill the gap left in her life by finding a young companion. The manager of the count's house in London "lent" her his eight-year-old daughter Mary Grove, who became part of Sally's household until she married a silversmith, Henry Gannell. Mary soon produced a daughter, Emma, and in 1827, when Sally (now fifty-three) was living in London at the house in Brompton Row and Emma was eighteen months old, the baby became Mary's replacement. She traveled everywhere with Sally on a joint passport that described them as "The Countess of Rumford and her niece Emma Rumford," and the pair eventually settled in America, where Emma married John Burgum in 1852, shortly before Sally died. But Emma also spent time with Victoire and her family, providing another source for the items she later wrote about the Rumford family.[1]

Just about the time Emma was becoming Sally's "niece," Sophie Baumgarten (now Madame de Miltez) died, in 1828, at the age of forty-four. Sally tells us that she died "in a mad-house in Geneva in Switzerland" as a result of an unfortunate marriage to a nobleman who treated her so badly as "first to destroy her health then her mind." But because she was already ill when Rumford visited Munich in 1810, the problems, whatever they were, seem to have been very deep rooted.

Charles Lefèvre also seems to have suffered mental ill health, although not so seriously as his half-sister. According to Emma, Rumford had arranged for Victoire to marry his gardener, a man named Bonnet, and provided them with money and a cottage.[2] M. Bonnet died in 1820, and Victoire moved to Paris with Charles, where Emma later got to know them quite well while living there with Sally.[3] She learned from them that Charles had worked so hard at school that when he was eleven years old he suffered a serious "brain fever" but recovered and did well at his studies. He originally thought of entering the priesthood, but when he decided instead on a military career Victoire had sufficient funds to purchase him a commission in the army.

This may have been a deliberate attempt to follow in his father's footsteps. Brought up on tales of Rumford's achievements, Charles, who bore a striking resemblance to his father, struggled long and hard to get legal recognition of his paternity. This may have contributed to what seems to have been a nervous breakdown that he suffered in 1843 or 1844, which led him to be temporarily confined in the asylum of Charendon. This was, by the standards of the day, an enlightened institution where artistic activities were encouraged, allowing Charles to make use of his talent for painting and skill at playing the piano. He seems to have made a full recovery, and after his release he returned to military duties and married in 1845. His wife, Pauline de Tauzier, was thirty at the time, and Merrill suggests that she must have been waiting for him during his illness and confinement. The couple had a son, Amédée Joseph (born in 1846), and at least one daughter, Marie Sarah (born in 1848). Charles eventually, in 1854, obtained the right to use the name Rumford, and he attained the rank of major, but died on September 8, 1855, in the last major battle of the Crimean War, a few weeks before his forty-second birthday. By then, Sally had been dead for nearly three years, but one of her last acts had been to ensure that the name Rumford did not die with him.

Sally was based in Auteuil after Rumford's death until May 1815, then moved to London.[4] Marie Lavoisier de Rumford gave up any claim on the house, but Sally remained there for only five years (collecting Mary Grove in the process) before returning to Paris, where she stayed until 1823. Then it was back to England until August 1835, when she went (now with Emma) to America. After almost exactly three years, she returned to Paris, and stayed there until July 1844 before finally (in her seventieth year) returning to Concord, where she died on December 2, 1852, at the age of seventy-eight.

Her will, made two years before her death, included a bequest of $10,000 to Amédée Lefèvre, then "about three years old," on condition that he "learns English, takes the name of Rumford, Lives at least part of the time here [that is, in America]." Amédée duly received the money, and adopted the name Rumford. But he never learned English, and never went to America. He joined the army, also reached the rank of major, married the splendidly named Berthe Marie Thérèse Rapine du Rozet de Ste Marie in 1872, but died when he was thirty-nine. He lived long enough, however, to correspond with Rumford's first biographer, George Ellis. In a letter dated February 21, 1883, he apologizes to Ellis for being unable to meet him at the Universal Exposition of 1878 in Paris because of illness, mentions that he has three daughters, and signs himself "A. de Rumford." Intriguingly, shipping records for 1908 show a passenger "Charles Oscard Marie de Rumford," born "about 1885," traveling from Bordeaux to New York, while in 1920 "Charles de Rumford," probably the same man, born "about 1883," sailed from Le Havre to New York. If this was the son of Amédée, he was the great-grandson of "our" Count Rumford, and takes the story of the Rumfords into the twentieth century, which is as far as we wish to go.

But what of Marie Lavoisier de Rumford? After Rumford's death she continued to be a leading society hostess, a "lady of the salon," as Ellis puts it. The nineteenth-century historian François Guizot tells us that in 1831

Madame de Rumford always assembled in her saloon Frenchmen and foreigners, savans, men of letters and men of the world, and always

assured for them alike around her table the interest of excellent con-
versation, as in her more numerous reunions the delight of the choicest
music.[5]

Marie died five years later, on February 10, 1836; Guizot continues:

I have witnessed as continuing and then passing away in the last of
the saloons of the eighteenth century. That of Madame de Rumford
was the last of them all. It closed in perfect consistency with itself,
without the entrance of any derangement, without passing through
any change unlike the tenor of its course. Madame de Rumford had
passed her life in the world, in seeking for herself and in offering to
others the pleasures of society.

That, of course, is why Rumford could not bear to live in the same house
with her. But he would have been delighted to know that long after he
had gone she was known by his name.

CODA

Rumford's Legacy

It has been said that Rumford's greatest discovery was Humphry Davy. It was thanks to Davy that the Royal Institution (RI) survived a difficult birth to become a thriving establishment, and it is possible that without him the institution might have failed. He carried out pioneering research in electrochemistry, initially using the powerful battery designed by Rumford, which alone would have ensured his scientific reputation; but he was also involved in promoting science, both through popular lectures and in the application of science to industry and agriculture, in ways that matched Rumford's vision of science in the service of humankind.

When Davy was appointed as a professor at the RI in 1802, he was still only twenty-three years old. His credentials as a scientist were cemented in 1806, when he gave the prestigious Bakerian Lecture of the Royal Society, presenting a review of the new science of electrochemistry that was so impressive that in 1807, in the midst of the Napoleonic Wars, the French Institute awarded him a medal and a cash prize of 3,000 francs. The work that made Davy famous involved passing electric currents through salts that were then known as caustic potash (potassium hydroxide) and caustic soda (sodium hydroxide). This liberated two previously unknown metals, which Davy named—potassium (from the potash) and sodium (from the soda). He later extended this work to "discover" magnesium, calcium, strontium, and barium.

From a modern perspective, the application of electricity from a battery in such experiments might seem a modest development, but in the first decade of the nineteenth century the apparatus Davy used was the equivalent of a modern-day particle accelerator and the discoveries were about as profound as those made by "atom smashers" like the ones at CERN, the European research laboratory in Geneva. In order to upgrade Davy's equipment in 1808, the RI had to raise funds by public subscription, and the end product was described by Davy[1] as consisting of

200 instruments, connected together in regular order, each composed of ten double plates, arranged in cells of porcelain, and containing in each plate thirty-two square inches; so that the whole number of double plates is 2,000, and the whole surface 128,000 square inches. This battery was charged with sixty parts water and one part nitric acid. It gave a spark from charcoal points through four inches of air.

In other work, Davy isolated and named chlorine, refined the definition of an element as a substance that cannot be decomposed by any chemical process, and established that the key component of all acids is not oxygen, as was previously thought, but hydrogen. Along the way, he discovered that when electricity was passed through a thin strip of charcoal the charcoal became so hot that it glowed; he had invented a form of electric light. Arguably, however, even these achievements as a scientific researcher were eclipsed at the time by Davy's other activities.

Over the ten years following his appointment, he gave popular lectures that packed the RI with fee-paying subscribers, many of them female fans of the darkly attractive young man with a way of making science sound exciting. His lectures were events like rock concerts today. They drew an audience from the fashionable strata of London society, including women who came to admire his looks and enjoy the sound of his voice, behaving in some ways like groupies. In order to avoid traffic jams at the time he was lecturing, Albermarle Street became the first one-way thoroughfare in London.

The success of the lectures was not down to luck. The physicist John Dalton gave a series of lectures at the RI in December 1803, and he has described how Davy prepared him for the event.[2] First, Dalton wrote out his first lecture in its entirety. Then Davy took him into the lecture theater, where Davy sat in the most distant corner of the hall to listen while

Dalton gave the entire lecture, after which he offered advice. "Next day," says Dalton, "I read it to an audience of about 150 to 200 people. . . . [T] hey gave me a very generous plaudit at the conclusion." At least at this point in his career, Davy was thorough and meticulous in his preparations, as well as being a natural showman.

But Davy's communication skills were not solely used to entertain the fee-paying public. He was an adviser to agriculture and industry,[3] and in one striking example gave a series of lectures on the application of chemistry to agriculture, which was so successful that in 1810 he repeated these talks, plus another series on electrochemistry, in Dublin, for a fee of 500 guineas. A year later, he gave another series of lectures in Dublin for 750 guineas—more than seven times his annual salary when he started at the RI. The Irish were so impressed that he was awarded the honorary degree of Doctor of Laws by Trinity College, Dublin—the only degree he ever received, but not his only honor. In 1812, Davy was knighted. He was the first person in Britain to be knighted for his scientific work—Isaac Newton received his knighthood for sordid political reasons, when he was standing as a member of Parliament, which had nothing to do with his science. Three days after being knighted, Davy married a wealthy widow. The same year, he resigned from the post of professor of chemistry at the RI (he was succeeded by William Brande), but stayed on as director.

By this time fame and fortune had turned Davy's head and he produced nothing else of any real importance before he died in 1829. But for all his achievements as an experimental scientist, one of his greatest achievements had been to rescue the RI from an early demise by his popular lectures.

If Humphry Davy was the greatest discovery that Count Rumford ever made, in the same vein it has also been said that the greatest discovery Humphry Davy ever made was Michael Faraday (1791–1867), whom he plucked from obscurity to become first his assistant and then his successor at the RI. Faraday started work at the RI in March 1813, exactly at the time Davy was losing interest in the nitty-gritty of being a serious scientific researcher. It was Faraday who ensured that the RI continued to flourish in the first half of the nineteenth century, both with popular lectures and with experimental science. If Davy ensured that the infant RI survived, Faraday ensured that the infant grew to independent adulthood.

Faraday was the archetypal example of a nineteenth-century autodidact. He came from a family too poor to obtain any formal education for him beyond the basics of reading, writing, and arithmetic, and as a teenager he worked as an apprentice to a bookbinder, where his passion for science was aroused by reading the books, including a third edition of the *Encyclopedia Britannica*, which were in the shop where he worked. He became a member of one of the many discussion groups organized at that time by young men wishing to "improve" themselves, where they discussed new discoveries, such as Davy's work on electrochemistry. In 1812, a customer at the shop gave Faraday tickets to attend what turned out to be the last lecture course Davy ever gave at the RI.

When his apprenticeship ended on October 7, 1812, Faraday found a job as a bookbinder, but wrote to anyone and everyone he could think of asking how to get a job in science. This eventually led to him being offered the job as Davy's assistant, with the warning from his new boss that "science [is] a harsh mistress, and in pecuniary point of view but poorly rewarding those who devote themselves to her service."[4] Davy was right. The pay was a guinea per week, plus accommodation at the top of the building on Albermarle Street. He was literally serving as Davy's bottle washer, as well as assisting in whatever experiments Davy did in his remaining time at the RI, and, as we saw in chapter 10, accompanying him to Paris and meeting Rumford later in 1813. Rumford can hardly have taken much notice of the young man at the time, but there was this brief direct contact between the man who founded the RI and the man who brought it to maturity.

In order to travel with Davy, Faraday had been forced to resign his post at the RI only six months after taking it up. But when he returned to England with Davy in May 1815 he was appointed as superintendent of the apparatus and assistant in the laboratory at an increased wage of 30 shillings per week, and with better rooms. From then on, he never looked back, growing in reputation as a scientist as Davy's activities declined. As he rose he was elected as a Fellow of the Royal Society in 1824, became the director of the laboratory in 1825, and the first Fullerian Professor of Chemistry at the RI in 1833—he had turned down a professorship at University College, London, in 1827. This is not the place to discuss Faraday's invention of both the electric motor and the electricity generator, let alone his ideas on electromagnetic fields and the nature of light.[5] More relevant to the legacy of Rumford was his innovation of the "Friday Evening Discourses" on science for a general audience, out of which grew his greatest contribution to scientific education, the Christmas Lectures for Children, which continue to the present day. Faraday's talks on "The Chemical History of a Candle," given in 1848, became a classic book that is still in print in various editions (although he married in 1821, Faraday had no children of his own).

Davy was flashy and drew attention to the RI just when it needed that kind of attention; Faraday was sound and serious, as well as being a good communicator, and built up an institution with its own traditions that was tough enough to survive without prima donnas. Faraday was a modest man, a member of the Sandemanian sect, who (unlike Rumford!) disapproved of honors and not only turned down the offer of a knighthood but twice declined the presidency of the Royal Society. He gave his last Friday Evening Discourse on June 21, 1862, and died on August 25, 1867, the last of the RI professors who had actually met Sir Benjamin Thompson, Count Rumford, Knight of the White Eagle, and scientific investigator of heat.

Notes

Prologue

1. *Philosophical Transactions*, volume LXXXVII, page 80.
2. His emphasis.
3. In the same way, an electric car can never be as fuel efficient as a car powered directly by petrol because the fuel has to be burned somewhere, then converted into electricity before the car can use it.
4. *Mémoires sur la Chaleur*.
5. *Heat Considered as a Mode of Motion* (Appleton, New York, 1871).

Introduction

1. *Sex and the Scientist*, by Jane Merrill; details of books cited are given in the sources and further reading.
2. See Bence Jones.

Acknowledgments

1. Confusingly, there is also a lesser work about Rumford by G. I. Brown; our references to "Brown" always mean Sanborn Brown unless otherwise specified.

Chapter 1

1. Unless otherwise specified, Thompson quotes are from Ellis, who wrote the first biography of Thompson and had access to many papers now lost, or the *Collected Works*.
2. It later became a restaurant, The Old Union Oyster House.
3. Adams, a lawyer, actually defended the soldiers at their trial; he was later the second president of the United States.
4. *Elementa Chemia*, published in 1732.
5. "Historical Review of the Various Experiments of the Author on the Subject of Heat," in the *Collected Works*.
6. Quoted by, among others, Sanborn Brown.

7. This was the same year that across the ocean in France the chemist Antoine Lavoisier married young Anne-Marie Paulze, who would feature significantly in Thompson's later life.

8. See note 7.

9. Quoted by Henry Bence Jones.

10. Familiar to readers of Jane Austen as the preferred mode of transport of slightly disreputable rich young men.

11. *Bibliothèque Britannique Sciences et Arts*, volume XVII (Geneva, 1801). Translation and other quotes from this source in Ellis.

12. Quoted by Sparrow.

CHAPTER 2

1. Letter in New Hampshire State Archives, quoted by Brown. Other quotes from New Hampshire archives from the same source.

2. Dispatch in Public Record Office, London.

3. It has been estimated that at the start of the troubles about a third of the colonists were loyal to the crown, a third actively opposed, and a third indifferent as long as they were left in peace. This highlights how easily the situation might have been resolved if the British had acted more reasonably.

4. There is some poetic license here about the chronology because shots had already been fired at Lexington, but Emerson prefers to commemorate a colonial victory rather than a defeat.

5. Washington was appointed to lead the army by the Second Continental Congress, held in Philadelphia on May 10, 1775; he was forty-three at the time.

6. See Ellis.

7. Achan was a biblical figure who was stoned to death for his sins.

8. Quoted by Brown.

9. See Ellis.

10. There is some doubt about the exact date; this is the one given by Ellis.

CHAPTER 3

1. F. Bickley, ed., *The Diaries of Sylvester Douglas (Lord Glenbervie)* (London: Constable, 1928).

2. George Ward, *The Journal and Letters of Samual Curwen* (New York: Francis, 1842).

3. After the resolution of the American conflict, on January 7, 1785, Jeffries, who had left America after his wife died in 1780 and set up practice in London, accompanied the French balloonist Jean-Pierre Blanchard on the first flight across the English Channel. He took with him a barometer, thermometer, and other instruments to make a scientific record of the conditions they encountered. They took two and a half hours to cross from Dover Castle to Guines, just south of Calais.

4. He became Sir Joseph two years later.

5. This was the fourth Earl of Sandwich, and the one after whom the food item is named.

6. Later Nelson's flagship. Thompson walked the same decks as Nelson, though not at the same time. In 1779 Nelson was in command of the brig *Badger*, cruising off Central America. As the *Victory* has been preserved at Portsmouth, and is open to the public, you can also follow in their footsteps.

7. Surely an exaggeration spread by rumor, but an indication of what people thought about him.

8. It was almost all practice. During Thompson's time with the fleet, there was one brief encounter with the combined French and Spanish forces, but Hardy promptly withdrew to safety in British ports.

9. According to a paper presented to the Royal Society in 1787; see *Collected Works*.

CHAPTER 4

1. Now in a position to do favors, Thompson arranged that the job went to Governor Wentworth's brother-in-law, John Fisher.

2. Letter in the Public Record Office.

3. Letter in the archive of the Royal Institution.

4. Charles King, ed., *The Life and Correspondence of Rufus King* (New York: Putnam's, 1896).

5. Originally Charlestown; the older spelling appears in some of the documents.

6. Quoted by Brown from a letter in the University of Michigan archive.

7. See Bence Jones.

8. As note 7.

9. See Sparrow.

10. As note 7.

11. Public Record Office, London.

12. See *The Correspondence of King George III*, ed. J. Fortescue (London: Macmillan, 1928).

13. See Bence Jones.

14. See Ellis.

15. Where John Wentworth was now surveyor general of the king's woods.

16. Letter in the Royal Institution archive.

CHAPTER 5

1. Letter in New Brunswick Museum, quoted by Sanborn Brown.

2. As note 1.

3. *The Autobiography and Correspondence of Edward Gibbon* (London: Alexander Murray, 1869).

4. The *Bibliothèque Britannique* was a monthly journal of the sciences and the arts published from 1796 to 1815.

5. As it turned out, after his brother died in 1799, Maximilian himself would succeed as elector of Bavaria.

6. Letter in the British Museum archive.

7. Public Record Office, FO9/3.

8. *The Winslow Papers*, ed. W. Raymond (St. John: New Brunswick Historical Society, 1901).

9. See the posthumous collection *Receuil des èleges historiques* (Paris: Didot, 1861).

10. Letter in the British Museum archive.

11. Brown says 1789.

12. *Count Rumford on the Nature of Heat*, ed. Sanborn Brown (London: Pergamon, 1967).

13. See Brown.

14. See the *Collected Works*.

15. Letter in the Public Record Office.

16. Quotes in this section without specific attribution are from articles in the *Collected Works*.

17. The "cuttings" were pieces of stale bread fried until they were crisp. Thompson had invented the crouton.

18. The Holy Roman Empire lasted until 1806, when the last emperor abdicated and was not replaced. But the title didn't die with it, and Thompson remained a count of a nonexistent empire.

CHAPTER 6

1. Letter in Public Record Office.

2. Through the Palmerstons, Rumford also met Lady Emma Hamilton, later the mistress of Lord Nelson.

3. Letter in Royal Society archive.

4. Letter in Royal Society archive.

5. Quoted by Brown.

6. See the *Collected Works*. To some extent Rumford's work duplicated earlier studies by Joseph Priestley, of which he was unaware at that time.

7. Letter in Royal Society archive, dated November 21, 1793.

8. Many of Rumford's letters to Lady Palmerston are now in the Dartmouth College archive; this is the source unless stated otherwise.

9. See *Collected Works*.

10. This "prophecy" was not as outrageous as it seems, because Count Baumgarten had died in 1790.

11. See the *Collected Works*.

12. See pages 144–45.

13. For bureaucratic and administrative reasons that are not relevant to Rumford's story, the American counterpart took longer to get going, but is also still in operation.

14. Munich's peace was short-lived, though. The city was occupied by the French in 1800, and by the Austrians in both 1805 and 1809.

15. See the *Collected Works*.

16. See Ellis.

17. Published in "Volume the Second" of his collection of essays, by Cadell and Davies.

18. That is, made more dense.

Chapter 7

1. See Bence Jones; other quotes in this section from that source unless otherwise indicated.
2. Quoted by Brown.
3. B. Connell, *Portrait of a Golden Age* (Boston: Houghton Mifflin, 1958).
4. See the *Collected Works*.
5. See Ellis.
6. His emphasis.
7. The royal seal was attached to the charter of the institution on January 13, 1800.
8. They actually started in February, as soon as the new lecture room was ready.
9. See *The Works of Peter Pindar, Esq.*, volume four (London: Keasley, 1802).
10. Copies of Rumford's letters to Pictet are held by the American Academy of Arts and Sciences.
11. Cavendish could afford to do this because he was immensely wealthy. He was once described as the richest of the wise, and the wisest of the rich.
12. Modern quantum theory incorporates elements of both ideas, in the form of "wave-particle duality."
13. Lord Palmerston died on April 16, 1802, and it is thought that she made the copy as a distraction from her grief. He had borrowed the original from his friend Pelham.
14. This hardly needs translating!

Chapter 8

1. Her given name is sometimes shortened to Marie (as is our choice) and sometimes to Anne.
2. See John West, *American Journal of Physiology* 305 (2013): 775.
3. Antoine's father died the same year.
4. See Guerlac.
5. See Riedman.
6. To complicate things further, in 1772 a third chemist, the Swede Carl Scheele, had also, unknown to Priestley or Lavoisier, independently discovered and studied the gas we now call oxygen.
7. Although Cavendish was then thirty-five, this was the first time he bothered to publish any of his discoveries.
8. Since June 1793, by the end of the Terror 16,594 death sentences had been passed throughout France, 2,639 of them in Paris.
9. See Merrill.

Chapter 9

1. See the *Collected Works*.
2. See Ellis.
3. Quoted by Bence Jones.
4. See the *Collected Works*.
5. And in the *Collected Works*.

6. Sweden was neutral at the time, but later joined the anti-Napoleon alliance.

7. See Ellis. By this time, Blagden and Rumford had fallen out, because Blagden felt that Rumford had not tried hard enough to defend his old friend against trumped-up charges of spying in 1803, which had made Blagden persona non grata in France, and the correspondence between them soon stopped. But Blagden remained on good terms with Sally, to whom he was now something of a father figure.

8. See Ellis.

9. See Bence Jones.

10. The question this raises is, why does water behave in this way? The answer lies outside the scope of the present book, but it has profound implications for human existence, which we have discussed elsewhere (John Gribbin, *Seven Pillars of Science* [London: Icon, 2020]). The description of Rumford's experiment is borrowed from there.

11. See Ellis.

12. Three days after the Battle of Trafalgar.

CHAPTER 10

1. A contemporary estimate gives the equivalent value of Rumford's pension at the time of his death as £1,200 per year; see Bence Jones.

2. See Ellis; all quotes from Sally's writings in this chapter are from that source.

3. A particular trial for Rumford, who ate very frugally and drank only water, because of his stomach problems.

4. Ellis.

5. Discussed in the coda.

6. Between three and four miles.

7. Under the Civil Code in force at the time, a couple could not divorce if the wife was older than forty-five, to protect her from being traded in for a younger model.

8. Bavaria would lose about thirty thousand men in Napoleon's Russian campaign, and eventually joined the coalition against Napoleon. Rumford was regarded as harmless and allowed to remain in Paris even after this.

9. Quoted by Brown.

10. Quoted by Brown.

11. The United States was officially neutral at this time, but friendly to France.

12. See the epilogue.

13. See the *Collected Works.*

14. War between Britain and the United States did not break out until June 1812.

15. Quoted by Brown.

16. See the *Collected Works.*

17. See John Paris, *The Life of Sir Humphry Davy* (London: Colburn & Bentley, 1831).

EPILOGUE

1. Including the brief history of Victoire's travel to Paris from Normandy mentioned in chapter 10.

2. It's worth noting that Rumford essentially lived with Victoire for five years, about as long as he spent with both his wives put together—two years with Sarah and three under the same roof with Marie.

3. Victoire married again in 1839, to a M. Antin, who died two years later. Charles was her only child.

4. Details of her travels come from Ellis.

5. François Guizot, *Mémoires pour servir à l'Histoire de mon Temps* (Paris, 1859). The "mémoire" about Marie was written originally in 1841.

CODA

1. See Bence Jones.

2. See Harold Hartley, *Humphry Davy* (London: Nelson, 1966).

3. Although the design of the famous "Davy lamp" for miners almost certainly owed a great deal to Faraday.

4. See Hartley.

5. See John and Mary Gribbin, *Faraday in 90 Minutes* (London: Constable, 1967).

SOURCES AND FURTHER READING

Bence Jones, Henry. *The Royal Institution, Its Founder and Its First Professors*. London: Longman, Green and Co., 1871; reprinted by Adamant Media Corporation, 2001.

Bradley, Duane. *Count Rumford*. Princeton: Van Nostrand, 1967.

Brown, G. I. *Count Rumford*. Stroud: Sutton, 1999.

Brown, Sanborn. *Benjamin Thompson, Count Rumford*. Cambridge, MA: MIT Press, 1979.

Brown, Sanborn, ed. *Collected Works of Count Rumford*. Cambridge, MA: Harvard University Press, 1970.

Brown, Sanborn, ed. *Count Rumford on the Nature of Heat*. London: Pergamon, 1967.

Donovan, A. *Antoine Lavoisier*. Cambridge, MA: Blackwell Scientific, 1993.

Dwight, C. Harrison. *Sir Benjamin Thompson, Count Rumford*. Cincinnati: Private edition, 1960.

Ellis, George. *Memoir of Sir Benjamin Thompson, Count Rumford, with Notices of His Daughter*. Boston: American Academy of Arts and Sciences, 1871.

Gillispie, Charles. *Pierre-Simon Laplace*. Princeton: Princeton University Press, 1997.

Guerlac, H. *Antoine-Laurent Lavoisier*. New York: Scribner's, 1975.

Guizot, François. *Madame de Rumford*. Paris: Crapèlet, 1841.

Hahn, Roger. *Pierre-Simon Laplace*. Cambridge, MA: Harvard University Press, 2005.

Hale, R. W. *Some Account of Benjamin Thompson*. Boston: Getchell and Son, 1927.

Larsen, Egon. *An American in Europe*. New York: Rider, 1953.

Martin, Thomas. *The Royal Institution*. London: RI, 1961.

Merrill, Jane. *Sex and the Scientist*. Jefferson: McFarland, 2018.

Poirier, Jean-Pierre. *La Science et l'Amour*. Paris: Pygmalion, 2004.

Riedman, Sarah. *Antoine Lavoisier*. New York: Nelson, 1957.

Rumford, Count. *The Complete Works*. American Academy of Arts and Sciences, four volumes, 1870–1873; English edition in five volumes, London: Macmillan, 1876.

Rumford, Count. *Mémoires sur la Chaleur*. Paris: Didot, 1804; reprinted by Hachette, 2014.

Sparrow, W. J. *Knight of the White Eagle*. London: Hutchinson, 1964.

Thompson, James. *Count Rumford of Massachusetts*. New York: Farrar and Rinehart, 1935.

Tyndall, John. *Count Rumford*. Clowes and Sons, 1883; reprinted by Kessinger, 2010.

Valentine, Alan. *Lord George Germain*. Oxford: Oxford University Press, 1962.

INDEX

Academy of Arts and Sciences, American, 84; Rumford Medal funded for, 98, 184n13

Academy of Arts and Sciences, Munich, 122

Academy of Sciences, Austria, 74

accomplishments, xv–xvi

Achan (biblical figure), 29, 182n7

Adams, John, 8, 181n3

adolescence, 6, 10–13; education in, 8–9; experiments during, 7

affairs: in Bavaria, 73–74, 105, 122; in France, 124–25. *See also* lovers

Aichner, Mary Sarah, 155, 158

Aichner family, 151, 154–55

ambassador, Bavarian, 106, 107

America: Academy of Arts and Sciences in, 84; return to, 108. *See also* colonies, in America; United States

Amiens, Peace of, 124

Appleton, John, 4–7

appointments, 107; in Bavaria, 74, 75, 78, 84, 102, 106, 107; in colonies, 14–15, 36, 45, 47; to count of the Holy Roman

Empire, 84–85; in Europe, 146; French, 124; of Regency Commandant, 100–101; to Royal Order of Saint Stanislaus (Knight of the White Eagle), 75; in Scotland, 116

apprenticeships, 4–7, 9–10; with Walker, T., 11

aristocracy, of Bavaria, ix, xiii, 83

army: reforms in Bavarian, 77–80; Russian, 169; of Washington, 25, 26, 27, 28, 182n5

Austen, Jane, 37, 98, 182n10

Austria: Academy of Sciences in, 74; siege of Munich by, 99–101

autism, 10

Bacon, Francis, xii–xiii

Baldwin, Cyrus, 29, 31

Baldwin, James, 163–64

Baldwin, Loammi, 7, 9, 111; correspondence with, 87–88, 94, 108; death of, 164; spying with, 26–28

ballistic pendulum, experiments with, 41–43

British secret service, rumors of
    spying by, 95
Brownian motion, 156–57
Burghausen, Frau von, advice
    from, 70
Burghausen, Heinrich Otto
    von, 70
Burgum, Emma, 171–72

Cadell and Davies (publisher), 95;
Philosophical Papers **and, 141**
caloric theory, of heat, 157;
    compared to kinetic theory,
    ix–x, xiii; Lavoisier, M., support
    of, 155
calorimeter, 166
Cambridge, Massachusetts, 9
Canada, Nova Scotia, 63
candle, standard, 82–83, 166
Candolle, Augustin de, 142
Canning, George, 107
cannons: boring experiments with,
    x–xii; flying artillery light, 109
Capen, Hopestill, 8
Carleton, Guy, 57–59; King's
    American Dragoons and,
    61–62
Carl Theodor (elector), 69, 99,
    107; death of, 109; peace with
    France and, 105–6; spying for,
    84; Thompson, B., and, 70–71,
    72–75, 101–2
Carolina, Charleston, 54–55
Castle Island, Massachusetts,
    25–26

cavalry officer, 57–58
Cavendish, Henry, 135, 185n7,
    185n11; phlogiston model and,
    136; RI and, 117
Charleston, Carolina, 54–55
Charlestown, Massachusetts, 22
chemistry, new, Lavoisiers
    and, 132
childhood, 3, 4–5, 6
children: Baumgarten, S., 73, 93,
    102–3, 122, 161; Lefèvre, C.,
    162, 168; Thompson, S., 16, 26,
    29–30, 76, 168–69
Church, Benjamin, 23;
    Washington and, 30
civil projects, in Bavaria, 79, 81
Clinton, Henry, 50; harassment by,
    53–55
coffee makers, invention of,
    159, 168
Collected Works (Thompson, B.), 44
colonies, in America, xiii;
    appointments in, 15, 36, 45,
    47; Battle of North Bridge, 24;
    birth in, 3; flight from, 29–31,
    62; Great Britain and, 5–11;
    raiding parties in, 56; return to,
    47, 53
colonists: army of, 25, 27; refugee,
    38, 46; taxation of, 5–7, 19;
    views on British rule of, 182n3
colors, of shadows, experiments
    on, 90–91, 184n6
combustion, theory of, 135

Yorktown, Virginia, Cornwallis in, 51, 54

Young, Thomas, 119–20